Our Medieval City! The First Jewish Community in Vienna

Our Medieval City! The First Jewish Community in Vienna

Published by Astrid Peterle, Adina Seeger, Domagoj Akrap, and Danielle Spera

Catalogue editors: Caitlin Gura-Redl, Agnes Meisinger

Jewish Museum Vienna

a museum of wienholding

Contents

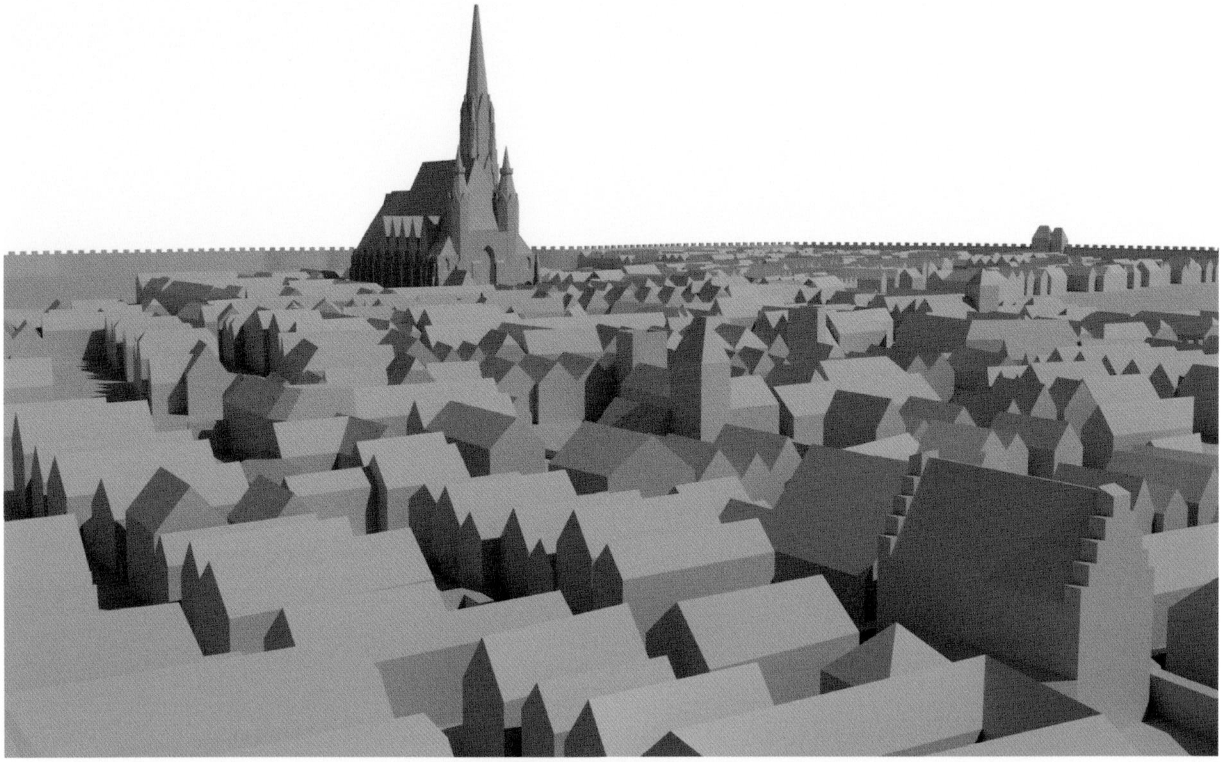

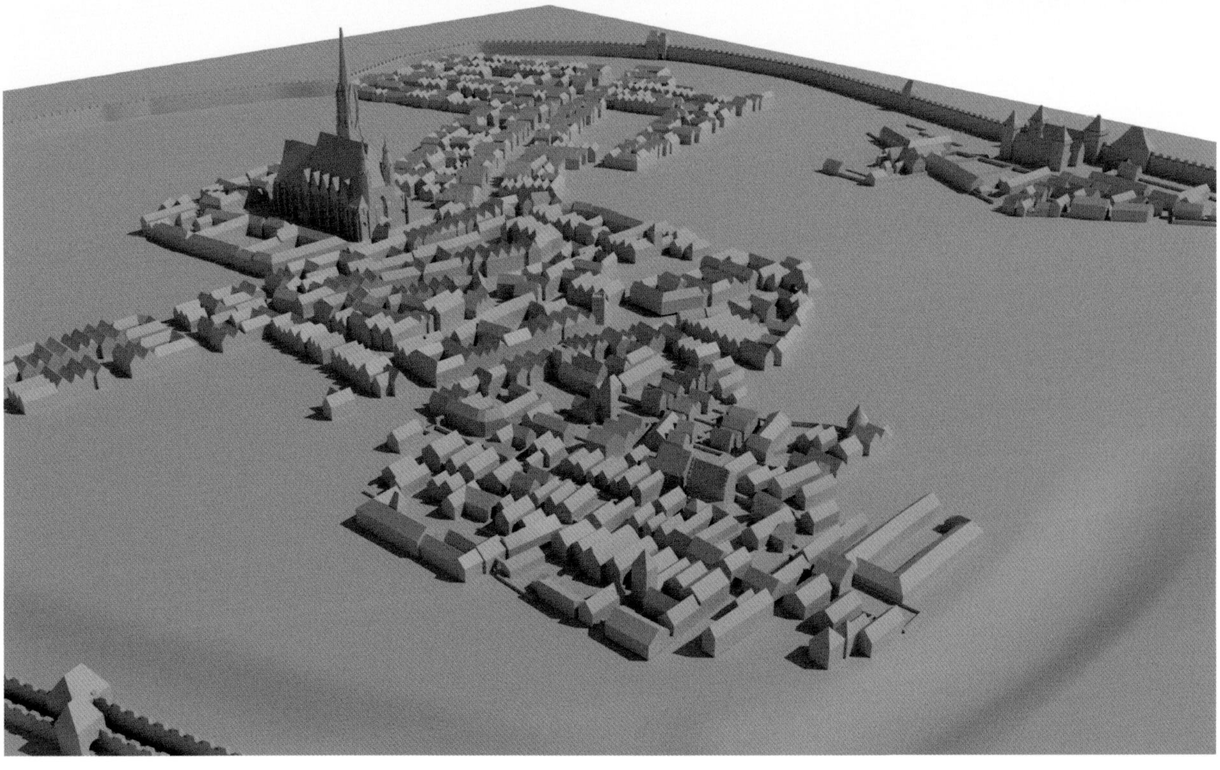

"A contribution in the fight against forgetting"

Judenplatz: a place where past, present, and future come together

Danielle Spera

Judenplatz is the best place to start understanding the Jewish history of Vienna, its present, and its future. It is the place where this history is compressed. The foundations of the medieval synagogue bear witness to the first Jewish community and its brutal destruction. A statue commemorates the important Enlightenment thinker Gotthold Ephraim Lessing. And the Shoah Memorial by the British artist Rachel Whiteread calls on everyone who crosses or pauses in the square to remember the Holocaust, the most terrible wound in Austrian Jewish history. Above all, however, Judenplatz is the home of a very active Jewish community, the Mizrachi, with a synagogue and a youth club. After the morning service, the Jewish worshippers, some with small children, leave the synagogue on Judenplatz. There is also a Catholic elementary school on the square, so that Jewish and non-Jewish children mingle around the Shoah Memorial. The recollection of the past offers hope for a peaceful present and future.

But back to history. The first Jew in Vienna to be recorded in documents was a man called Schlom, who lived in the late twelfth century. He was summoned to Vienna by the Babenberg Duke Leopold V (1157–1194) and appointed mint master, just after Leopold had received the ransom in the form of silver bars for release of the English king Richard the Lionheart. Schlom was given the task of minting coins from the silver. He owned

3D renderings for the model of medieval Vienna, designed by 7reasons Medien GmbH in consultation with Paul Mitchell, 2020

property in Vienna in the area of today's Seitenstettengasse. His family and staff formed a small Jewish community, which also had a synagogue. Schlom employed Christians as well. His life came to a violent end in 1196. One of his Christian employees stole from him and Schlom had him arrested. The wife of the thief informed some crusaders, who massacred Schlom and fifteen other Jews. Duke Frederick I (1175–1198), the son of Leopold V, had the ringleaders executed.

From the thirteenth century, Jews settled in the area around the present-day Judenplatz. At this time, Vienna was gaining in importance as the Babenberg ducal residence. The Jewish quarter with the synagogue at its center developed along today's Wipplingerstrasse, at the time an important trade and transit route. It was not a ghetto, in that no one was forced to live there. The Jewish and Christian communities cohabited peacefully and productively without any major conflicts. Vienna became the home of a flourishing Jewish community, which by the following century was one of the largest and most important in Europe.

At the same time, a community infrastructure developed, with a slaughterhouse, bakery, school, hospital, bathhouse, probably a mikveh, and a cemetery just outside Vienna's Kärtnertor gate. The Jewish quarter had around nine hundred inhabitants, five percent of the city's population. Following the plague pogroms that destroyed Jewish communities in Germany, Vienna became a center of Jewish scholarship. Apart from the religious authorities, there were also tailors, shoemakers, butchers, midwives, and doctors. Judenplatz, then called the "Schulhof" (from the Yiddish "shul," meaning synagogue or place of learning, and the German word "Hof" = courtyard), was the focal point of the city's Jewish life in the Middle Ages. At its heart was an imposing late-medieval synagogue, built in the mid-thirteenth century, probably by cathedral architects, and extended over the next 150 years to become one of the largest synagogues of its time.

This religious, cultural, and economic heyday came to a traumatic end with the expulsion and massacre of the Jews of Vienna in 1420/21. Claims that the Viennese Jews had supported the Hussite movement, coupled with Duke Albert V's need for funds in order to marry the daughter of the Holy Roman Emperor Sigismund, are thought to have triggered the act of violence that extinguished the entire community. Two hundred wealthy

Depiction from a Hebrew codex of the construction of a city. The houses of the Jewish quarter are crowded together in the lower town near the city walls, Germany, c. 1428.

Jews were burnt at the stake in Erdberg on March 12, 1421, and the rest were set adrift on the Danube in rudderless boats. The synagogue was demolished and the stones used in the construction of the University of Vienna. After the Jewish community had been exterminated, the "Schulhof" was renamed "Judenplatz."

Over the centuries, the history of the medieval Viennese Jewish community was forgotten. There was nothing left to recall the important Jewish medieval past and its brutal end, and it is only through archaeological and historical research that this story has gradually been brought to light again.

In the early twentieth century, Vienna wanted to commemorate the German Enlightenment author Gotthold Ephraim Lessing. In 1935, a statue

Oswald Redlich, member of the State Council and president of the Academy of Sciences, speaking at the unveiling of the Lessing monument on Judenplatz in 1935

of him was erected on Judenplatz, created by the Austrian sculptor Siegfried Charoux, who emigrated to Britain soon afterwards. In 1939, the statue was removed by the Nazis and melted down. After World War II, Charoux was again commissioned to design a Lessing monument, but did not live to see it unveiled on Vienna's Morzinplatz, from where it was eventually moved back to Judenplatz in 1981. In the last decades of the twentieth century, Judenplatz deteriorated into an unattractive square usually full of parked cars.

In the late 1980s, during the public debate concerning the wartime past of Austrian Federal President Kurt Waldheim, the idea arose to create commemorative sites in Vienna. As a result, the sculptor Alfred Hrdlicka was commissioned in 1988 to design a memorial against war and fascism. The figure of a Jew scrubbing the sidewalk, which formed part of the monument, gave rise to considerable criticism. It was misinterpreted and used as a bench, whereupon the artist surrounded it with barbed wire, which caused even further heated criticism.

During this discussion, Simon Wiesenthal, a tireless campaigner for justice, called on the City of Vienna to create a memorial to the Austrian Jews murdered in the Holocaust. He was able to gain the support of Michael Häupl, mayor of Vienna at the time, and suggested Judenplatz as a suitable location. Opposition quickly emerged, both from the Jewish community and the Church. A protest initiative supported by the Freedom Party of Austria (FPÖ) lamented the loss of parking space and expressed concerns that the memorial would attract graffiti or become a target for attacks. The project had not even fully begun but was already lambasted by the media, which referred to it as the "Jewish monument" and "Jewish discussion."

When an international jury chose the design by the British artist Rachel Whiteread, a new wave of protest arose. One of Wiesenthal's conditions had been that the memorial should be abstract. Although all entries complied with this, the jury was swayed by Whiteread's design of a hollow concrete cube with closed doors and rows of identically sized books with their spines facing inward—a monument that also symbolizes the emptiness left behind by the Holocaust. When the winning entry was announced, many commentators were enraged. The proposed monument was described as a "concrete carbuncle" or even compared by one district chairperson to the entrance of a public toilet.

Archaeological excavations on Judenplatz, 1996

Then, during the preparations in 1995 for the installation of the memorial, the unexpectedly extensive foundations of the medieval synagogue were unearthed. This exciting find led to renewed discussion on how to proceed. Once again, endless debate ensued, now also involving rabbis, who argued that no structure should be erected on top of the former synagogue. Suggested alternatives included the construction of a glass roof over the excavated synagogue. After a long tug-of-war, it was decided initially to move the memorial closer toward the center of the square. It is hardly surprising, after all these protracted discussions, that today the artist no longer wishes to speak much about the project.

Eventually the decision was made to erect the memorial above the excavations after all. For this to happen, the remains of the synagogue had to be lowered in a highly complex engineering maneuver. A display area was created in the basement of the Mizrachi House to make the excavations accessible via a passage. The Mizrachi House itself has had an interesting history: in medieval times it was inhabited by a Viennese Jewish family; then, centuries later, it once again came into Jewish ownership. Today it belongs to the Mizrachi, an orthodox Zionist association within the Jewish community. During the redevelopment of Judenplatz, this building was also refurbished. The exhibition rooms on its ground floor, in the basement, and the adjacent remains of the medieval synagogue were entrusted to the Jewish Museum by the City of Vienna.

The permanent exhibition was updated only once thereafter and, twenty years after its opening, no longer reflected the current status of research. We therefore decided to develop a completely new concept, involving experts from a wide range of disciplines. Among other things, it was important for us to debunk some of the still extant myths and interpretations of the medieval era as the Dark Ages. Another imperative was accessibility. Inclusion was the watchword, with a particular focus on children and on the museum as a place for questions and answers, for communication and contemplation, in keeping with the dignity of this important Jewish and historical site, which in 2000 had been so elegantly and sensitively designed by architects Jabornegg & Pálffy.

The new exhibition concept was implemented by head curator Astrid Peterle and Adina Seeger, who was also responsible for coordinating the project. After the departure of Werner Hanak, on whose initial ideas the new concept was based, Peterle and Seeger, together with Domagoj Akrap, Anna Lidor-Osprian, and Janine Zettl, curated the new permanent exhibition. Caitlin Gura-Redl provided energetic support in the production

Medieval-themed Advent market in front of the Museum of Military History in Vienna, 2019

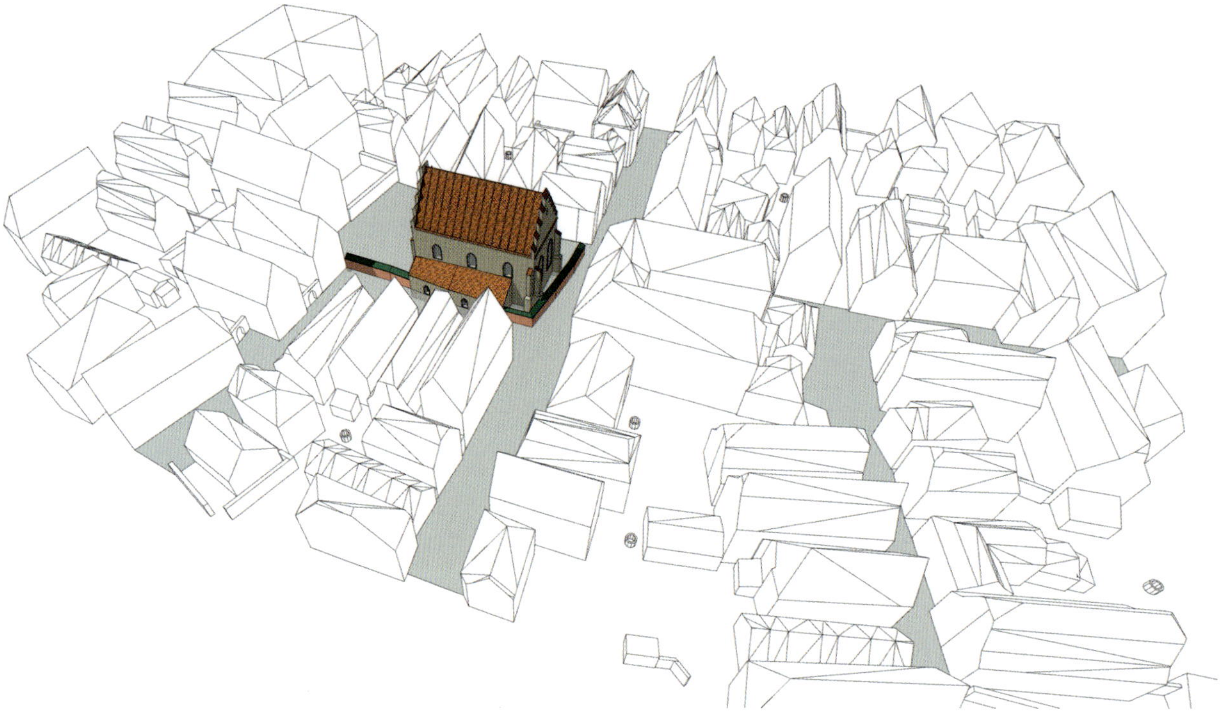

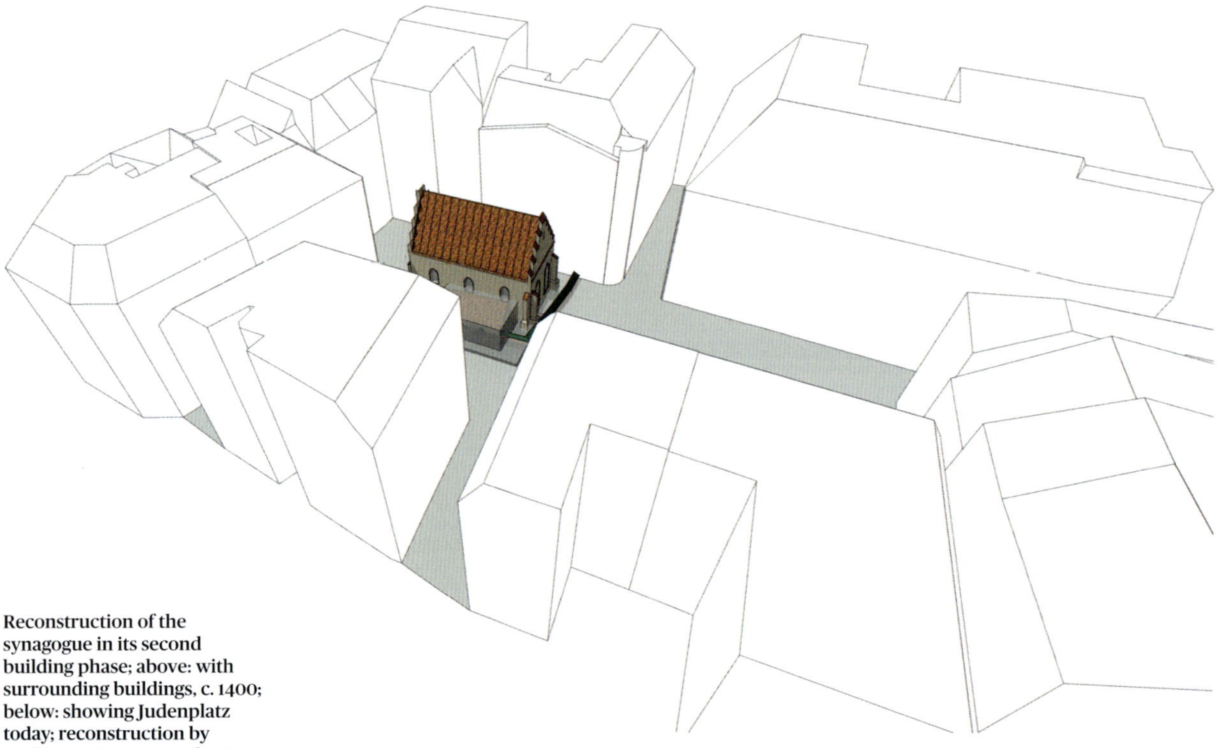

Reconstruction of the synagogue in its second building phase; above: with surrounding buildings, c. 1400; below: showing Judenplatz today; reconstruction by Herbert Peter in consultation with Paul Mitchell, 2020

of the exhibition. I thank them all most sincerely. The development of the curatorial concept for the exhibition was overseen by an expert advisory board: Martha Keil, director of the Institute for Austrian Jewish History, Thomas Kühtreiber, Institute for Medieval and Early Modern Material Culture at the University of Salzburg, and Christina Lutter, professor of Austrian history at the University of Vienna. We are grateful to them for their support and their helpful and motivating feedback. I thank Paul Mitchell, who was also deputy head of the excavations in the 1990s, for his competent and knowledgable assistance regarding archaeology and building research. Herbert Peter showed great ingenuity in the technical design and implementation of the virtual reconstruction of the synagogue, using an augmented reality application to visualize all its building phases, which can now be viewed in the exact place where the synagogue originally stood.

The impressive new model of the medieval city was designed by 7reasons. Paul Mitchell is again to be thanked for contributing his expertise, and the WIEN MUSEUM for its generous support. Together with Tactile Studio and Herbert Peter, we also developed tactile objects for blind and sight-impaired visitors.

Hannah Landsmann conceived the integrated education program, which was implemented with great dedication by Dominikus Guggenberger. Thanks are due to Roland Plachy for the illustrations, and to Anna Artaker and Andrew M. Mezvinsky for their superb artistic contributions. Josef Gaschnitz was the commercial manager (having taken over in May 2020 from Markus Roboch), with Claudia Lauppert responsible for accounts. Bettina Dräxler oversaw conservation aspects, Cornelia Regehr the registrar's office, Christa Prokisch and Katharina Lischka the archive, and Sabine Frank the literature research. Petra Fuchs handled PR and social media, and Ida Salamon looked after sponsoring und marketing. I thank them all most sincerely.

The exhibition layout was designed by Gerhard Abel and Dawit Kassaw from PLANET architects and Stefan Fuhrer, who was also responsible for all graphic design work for the exhibition, the catalogue, and other printed material. Severin Mahrer, our technical manager, skillfully coordinated the accessibility improvements, the installation of a new air conditioning system and Anna Artaker's artistic intervention, as well as the entire

St. Stephen's Cathedral (underlit), in contrast to the much smaller synagogue; model of medieval Vienna, designed by 7reasons Medien GmbH in cooperation with Paul Mitchell, November 2020

redesign of the exhibition areas. The audiovisual media were created by Florian Prix and Hannes Köcher from cat-x exhibitions. Patrick Topitschnig was responsible for the video interviews, film production, and editing, Tom Juncker for the sound editing of the audio commentaries, and Elisa Heinrich for the transcriptions.

My thanks for the production of this catalogue go to Agnes Meisinger and Caitlin Gura-Redl. We are delighted and grateful to have been able to obtain some highly informative contributions from renowned experts in their fields: Nora Berend, Mika Boros and Alexandra Hylla, Eveline Brugger and Birgit Wiedl, Petr Elbel and Wolfram Ziegler, Martha Keil, Thomas Kühtreiber, Anna Lidor-Osprian, Klaus Lohrmann, Paul Mitchell, Simon Neuberg, and Siegrid Schmidt. Translation and editing of the catalogue and exhibition texts were undertaken by Nick Somers, Vera Ribarich, Verena Pawlowsky, Betti Moser, and Saskia Haag. We thank Böhlau Verlag, particularly Waltraud Moritz and Ursula Huber, for their support in this.

Special thanks are due to the WIEN MUSEUM, which loaned the objects on display, and to its director Matti Bunzl, financial director Christina

Schwarz, and head of objects in the curatorial department Michaela Kronberger for their assistance. I also thank the City Archaeology Department headed by Karin Fischer Ausserer.

My gratitude goes to all interview partners involved in the design of Judenplatz in the late 1990s for sharing their fascinating memories.

The redesign of the permanent exhibition would not have been possible without public and private financial support. From the outset, the former minister for arts and culture Thomas Drozda was enthusiastic about our ideas, as was Daniel Löcker, section head in Vienna's Municipal Department for Cultural Affairs (MA 7). I want to thank them most sincerely for their unstinting support of our project. Thanks also to the National Fund of the Republic of Austria for Victims of National Socialism and its secretary general Hannah Lessing. My special thanks go also to the Rothschild Foundation Hanadiv Europe, as well as Michael Brenner and Christian Rapp for their support, Stefan Ottrubay and the pancivis stiftung, feratel media technologies AG and Markus Schröcksnadel, Christiane Wenckheim and Ottakringer Getränke AG, and Gerhard Starsich and Münze Österreich AG (Austrian Mint). Working together with the museum, the Austrian Mint produced a special set of commemorative euro coins in honor of Vienna's first mint master Schlom. The bimah, the podium from which the Torah is read, is the center of every synagogue. The floor plate showing the shape of the medieval bimah on Judenplatz was installed with generous support from the US Friends of the Jewish Museum Vienna. Furthermore, I would like to thank the Chamber for Workers and Employees, in particular its director Christoph Klein and Roman Berka, the Friends of the Jewish Museum Vienna, the Mark and Melissa Simon Fund, Prof. Stefan Stolitzka, Josef Ostermayer and Hausservice Objektbewirtschaftungs GmbH, NITSCH FOUNDATION, as well as the Zumtobel Group.

Judenplatz is an extraordinary place in many respects. To this day, you can still find an inscription on one of its buildings that celebrates the murder of Jews in the Middle Ages. On another building, belonging to the Catholic Church, is a plaque that draws attention to the complicity of many clergymen and priests in the medieval antisemitism. The wording of this text, too, was the subject of lively discussion, not least in a fascinating—and for me extremely memorable—exchange in my own living room, involving Archbishop Cardinal Christoph Schönborn and a group of friends.

The realization of Simon Wiesenthal's idea has created a place of memory that is unparalleled in Europe. It combines Rachel Whiteread's Memorial to the Austrian Jewish Victims of the Shoah, the archaeological remains of the medieval synagogue, and Museum Judenplatz, where the life of the Viennese Jews in the Middle Ages is now being shown in a completely new light—an extraordinary ensemble.

I personally regard Judenplatz with the memorial and the excavations of the medieval synagogue as the most important Jewish site in Vienna—a place that, as a result of its history, but also its present and future perspectives, has become imbued with an almost spiritual aura.

Responding to the concern about the memorial becoming a target for antisemitic graffiti, the artist Rachel Whiteread said: "A few daubed swastikas on it would really make people think about what is happening in their society, their culture. I certainly don't want to encourage it, but if it happens, it happens."[1] So far, these fears have proved to be unfounded, and we hope that this will remain so in the future.

After years of wrangling, the memorial on Judenplatz was officially unveiled on October 25, 2000. Simon Wiesenthal said at the time: "The memorial will name the victims and accuse the perpetrators. These sentences stand for fifty years of my life's work. The entire Judenplatz will encourage people to reflect, to read and learn, and it will be a contribution in the fight against forgetting."[2] This objective has been achieved in the best possible sense.

Unveiling of the Memorial to the Austrian Jewish Victims of the Shoah, designed by Rachel Whiteread, Judenplatz, October 25, 2000

SITZ-u.STEHBEISL
ZUM „SCHERER"

Skeleton of a dog, found during the excavations on Judenplatz in the second half of the 1990s in the well of a medieval house near the site of the present-day Lessing monument

Forward from the Present to the Past

The new permanent exhibition at Museum Judenplatz

Astrid Peterle

One of the sensational finds during the archaeological excavations on Judenplatz in the second half of the 1990s, along with the remains of the medieval synagogue destroyed in 1421, was the skeleton of a small whippet-like dog. It was found in the well of a Jewish house in the area of today's Lessing monument. An archaeozoological examination provided further information, for example, that it had sustained serious injuries but had been nursed back to health and that it died around 1380.[1] How and why it fell into the well of a Jewish house will remain a mystery. Were animal carcasses usually disposed of in that way in those days? What was a dog doing in the Jewish quarter at all, given that these animals are considered unclean in Jewish law and for that reason are not kept as pets by strictly religious Jews? Could it have been an attempt to poison the well? Anti-Jewish hostility in the Middle Ages included accusations of well-poisoning. Was this anti-Jewish animosity turned around and a dog thrown into a "Jewish" well as an act of revenge? The skeleton, which is on display in the exhibition, illustrates how historical objects can provide us with factual information, but at the same time give rise to more unanswered questions, different interpretations and speculation, and how we project our modern-day emotions onto them. The questions and theories connected with this find are an example of the approach to the past we have generally adopted in our new concept for the permanent exhibition.

Many layers of the Jewish history of Vienna, from the Middle Ages to the present day, can be found on Judenplatz. Jews settled here in the early thirteenth century, forming the basis for the first community, which over the course of the following two hundred years developed to become one of the most important in Central Europe. In 1420/21 it was systematically obliterated by order of Duke Albert V, and the central synagogue on Judenplatz destroyed. After this tragic and sudden end to the community, known as the Vienna Gesera, all awareness of the Jewish history of this site disappeared from the city's memory for centuries. It was not until the 1990s—during the project for a memorial to Austrian Jewish victims of the Shoah and as a result of the excavation of the remains of the destroyed medieval synagogue—that the significance of this site in the city's history was once again revealed and discussed. Today, Judenplatz is not only a place of memory in the heart of the city but also a vibrant urban space and central focus of modern-day Jewish life, with an active synagogue and youth club and, since 2000, a second branch of the Jewish Museum Vienna.

In view of the multifaceted nature of history, Museum Judenplatz is the ideal space not only to narrate the beginnings of Jewish life in this city but also to reflect on the process of historiography, research, and museology. The permanent exhibition extends far beyond the past; it relates the biography of this site up to the present day and invites visitors to participate in its rediscovery.

The key

One of the main symbols of this "unlocking of history" in the exhibition is, quite literally, a key. During the excavations on Judenplatz in the late 1990s, a medieval key was found at the foot of the entrance steps into the synagogue. It stands for many of the questions and challenges of historical research. We don't know what it locked or unlocked. It would have been nice if it had come with a tag saying "synagogue" or "mikveh" (ritual bath), "butcher," or the like. It might have been lost by someone who had a house, store, or workshop close by; it could have belonged to a Jew or a Christian, or even a traveler passing

Iron key found among the remains of the destroyed synagogue during the excavations on Judenplatz in the second half of the 1990s

through. The fact is, we don't know and we never will. Like the dog mentioned earlier, the key reminds us how objects can be charged with historical significance. In the design of the exhibition, we have used it as a symbol to mark "key moments," where we give visitors an insight into the work of a curator/researcher and offer information about the kinds of questions historians ask, their research methods, and the interrogation of historical sources.

Throughout the exhibition there are also "keyholes." They mark points where we question clichés about the Middle Ages in general. This "keyhole view" of the bigger picture is important in connection with the specific question of Jewish life in the Middle Ages, which cannot be separated from the living conditions and realities of the Christian majority society. There are so many modern-day preconceptions about the Middle Ages that simply do not stand up to academic scrutiny. These clichés took root, above all, during the Romantic era in nineteenth-century Europe.[2] By considering medieval Vienna from a specifically Jewish perspective—for the most part ignored, suppressed, and forgotten—we may also be able to recalibrate our familiar assumptions and misconceptions about this period in history.

Confronting the gaps

In the exhibition, we ask questions about the past that don't necessarily have—or need—answers. History should always be considered in the plural; in other words, we can never tell a single, generally valid history, but are always dealing with multilayered histories, related from different perspectives, for different reasons, and with different aims. We consider the history of medieval Vienna from a Jewish point of view. This also means that we have to have the courage to accept that there will be gaps. In present-day Vienna, the Middle Ages are an underrepresented era. The city lives to a large extent from its nostalgic image as a world center of art and culture, particularly "Vienna 1900," a period in which the significant contribution of Jews to the city's history is only now being fully acknowledged. Most physical traces of medieval Vienna fell victim to the desire of generations of Habsburg emperors to leave their mark on the capital city by erecting ever more grandiose buildings. Soon after the massacre and expulsion

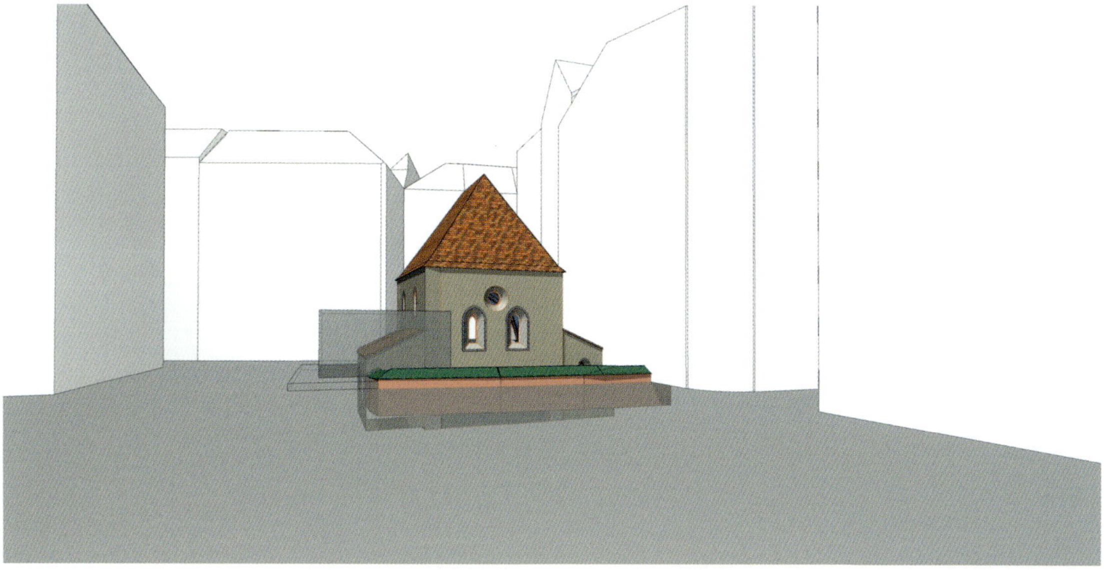

of the Jewish community in the fifteenth century, its contribution to the late medieval history of the city was not only visibly and materially expunged but also suppressed in the city's memory. This not only meant that many sources—be it buildings, objects, or documents—have not survived, but also that for many centuries the few remnants that still existed were not researched or made visible. We draw attention to these gaps in the cultural awareness of the city and in academic circles and show how we acquire our knowledge about Jewish life in the Middle Ages: what sources, documents, and objects there are, what they can tell us, what questions we can ask of the past, what answers can be found for certain, and what questions will perhaps remain unanswered forever. We also wanted to make known some of the historical protagonists who had remained invisible until now because they were ignored by historians for a long time. In our narrative, for example, we highlight the stories of Jewish women who are on record as having been successful in business or as scribes.

Reconstruction of the first phase (1240–50) of the medieval synagogue, showing its position on Judenplatz near the present-day memorial. It clearly illustrates the difference in surface level between the square as it is today, the medieval building, and the archaeological display room. This 2020 reconstruction of the synagogue, created by Herbert Peter assisted by Paul Mitchell, is hypothetical: some aspects are evident from the foundations, but other details, such as the windows and roof, are modeled on comparable buildings from the same era.

Without archaeology and building research, we would know much less about Judenplatz and Vienna's Jewish community. It is thanks to these disciplines, combined with Simon Wiesenthal's initiative, the political will and the commitment of civil society in the 1990s, that Museum Judenplatz exists today. We therefore focus particularly on these two disciplines and draw attention to their contributions to research, particularly on the synagogue. We were fortunate to acquire the services of the archaeologist and building researcher Paul Mitchell. From 1995 to 1998, he was deputy head of the archaeological excavations on Judenplatz—a project that was considered pioneering in Viennese urban archaeology at the time—and has since been responsible for numerous research projects on the topography and history of the medieval Jewish quarter, which also informed the exhibition.

For many years, the Viennese architect Herbert Peter has been conducting research on the synagogues in Vienna destroyed by the Nazis during the November Pogrom in 1938. For our exhibition, he created a reconstruction of the medieval synagogue on Judenplatz, now shown in the excavation display area. Utilizing augmented and virtual reality, it gives a highly realistic impression of the various construction phases and spatial proportions, all brought to life at the original location of the synagogue.

Allowing objects to speak

For historical objects like those found during the archaeological excavations on Judenplatz to really speak to us, we must recreate the link to the site where they were found, while at the same time placing them in a wider context. Many of the objects found during the Judenplatz excavations, with the exception of the remains of the synagogue, give no indication of a Jewish or religious context. We therefore focus on the meaning of these finds in a general medieval context and explore the shared everyday culture of the minority and majority societies. The objects make clear that, in contrast to later centuries, the medieval Jewish quarter was not an involuntary settlement—like the seventeenth-century ghetto in Unterer Werd, for example—but an urban site of cohabitation, where Christians and Jews interacted professionally and economically, and lived, celebrated, and conducted their business side by side. In the exhibition, objects such as drinking vessels, a comb, and a stylus, but also dice and game tokens, bear witness to this shared everyday culture. Equally, the coins found on Judenplatz can provide a starting point for fascinating stories, helping us to date associated finds and providing information about medieval travel—or proving to be contemporary forgeries.

Everyday objects found during the excavations on Judenplatz in the second half of the 1990s, from l. to r.: fragments of a medieval comb, fragment of a toy horse, the upper part of a stylus, and the panels of a mirror frame

A site with many levels of meaning

The archaeological display area is the heart of Museum Judenplatz. The remnants of the synagogue destroyed in 1421 bear vivid witness to the persecution, expulsion, and murder of the members of Vienna's first Jewish community. But they are also evidence of the life of an important and vibrant community that existed on this site for almost two hundred years. The main exhibition room, before entering the archaeological display area, therefore contains detailed information about Vienna's medieval community, its significance for Jewish culture and religion, its institutions, and also the personalities whose stories we are able to retrace today: from mint master Schlom and the businesswoman Plume to major scholars such as Rabbi Isaac ben Moses, known as Or Zarua, whose writings are still highly respected by orthodox Jewry today.

In order to highlight the multiple significance of the site, the chapters on the Vienna Gesera and anti-Judaism come after the archaeological display area. We deliberately address the theme of anti-Judaism at the point where the exhibition transitions from the Middle Ages to the early modern period in order to emphasize the continuity.

The available sources on the Vienna Gesera do not give a clear explanation of Albert V's motives, particularly since there are no documents written from his own personal perspective. Some of the more recent interpretations on this topic have given rise to controversy. In the exhibition, we present various interpretations to demonstrate how historical research and history must be seen as an ongoing work in progress. In this catalogue, five reputed academics and scholars answer the same questions on the Gesera in quite different ways, depending on their disciplines and particular perspectives.

There is no question that the expulsion and murder of the first Jewish community marked a tragic and brutal disruption. Nevertheless, we did not want to end the exhibition with the Vienna Gesera and the chapter on anti-Judaism, but have continued the story of Jewish life in Vienna after 1420/21. Visitors will learn about the traces of Jewish life in Vienna in the two hundred years between the Vienna Gesera and the ghetto in Unterer Werd. From the biography of the Judenplatz site and its history between 1421 and 1995, the exhibition leads on to the unveiling of Rachel Whiteread's memorial and the opening of the museum in the year 2000. It looks at the heated and protracted political and public debate on the memorial design, the Judenplatz site itself, and the incorporation or non-incorporation of the archaeological finds in the memorial concept. Interviews with the stakeholders at the time give an insight into these controversies.

Our Middle Ages!

The title of our new permanent exhibition is a statement, an admonition, and a mandate, all rolled into one. In a city in which right up to the present day the Middle Ages have played a subordinate role in the contemplation of history and culture, we invite visitors to join us in taking a look at Vienna from what may seem like a new perspective. The "our" in the title refers to several positions of ownership: that of the medieval Jews, who considered Vienna their home and whose lives were extinguished, forgotten, and suppressed; that of the museum, which looks at the life of the first Jewish community in Vienna through this exhibition; and that of our visitors, who embark on this journey together with us and who also shape history through their own experiences. The title also links back to the permanent exhibition opened in 2013 at Palais Eskeles, entitled *Our City! Jewish Vienna—Then to Now*.

In recent years, museums have been thankfully taking more and more measures to be as inclusive as possible. In line with this trend, the new permanent exhibition at Museum Judenplatz has been designed to be completely barrier-free. The exhibition content is also designed to allow for incremental additions over time to ensure inclusiveness. As a first step, some of the stations in the exhibition tour, such as the model of the Jewish quarter and of Rachel Whiteread's memorial, feature tactile elements. They should be understood as an enriching feature for all visitors, whether they are sight-impaired or not.

We also offer integrated elements for families and different age groups. These features were developed in close collaboration with Hannah Landsmann, head of the education department at the Jewish Museum Vienna. Along with stations for our youngest visitors, a room at the end of the exhibition trail offers an opportunity to stop and reflect, to browse this catalogue, and to have a go at solving a puzzle

Visualization of the architecture for the new permanent exhibition at Museum Judenplatz, PLANET architects, 2020

addressing some of the everyday themes that occupied members of medieval Jewish communities and playfully suggesting that some of them were not so different from those that preoccupy us today.

Our exhibition!

Curating a permanent exhibition is probably one of the greatest and most exciting challenges in a curator's career. I would like to thank Danielle Spera for giving me this opportunity and for entrusting me with this project, for her untiring commitment and enthusiasm for the theme, and for the fruitful dialogue. I would also like to thank my predecessor Werner Hanak, who started the project and provided important stimuli. I am extremely grateful to my wonderful colleagues who have assisted me in creating this exhibition: Domagoj Akrap, Adina Seeger, and Janine Zettl. Thank you for your commitment, curiosity, and willingness to take innovative approaches. My thanks also go to Anna Lidor-Osprian for her enthusiasm and her wide-ranging Jewish medieval expertise, to Adina Seeger, who has tirelessly coordinated the project from the outset, always with a precise eye on the schedule, and to Caitlin Gura-Redl, who took on the exhibition production in the second half of the project with impressive energy and attention to detail. I thank Hannah Landsmann for helping us develop the integrated education program and for her openness to experimentation. I am grateful to Markus Roboch, our former commercial manager, and his successor Josef Gaschnitz, for their enthusiastic commitment to the exhibition theme while also keeping a strict eye on the budget, and to Claudia Lauppert for keeping the accounts.

A permanent exhibition is a joint project involving many people. The ongoing exchange with experts from the various disciplines involved in researching the history of Judenplatz and Vienna's first Jewish community has been particularly important to us. Our special thanks go to archaeologist Paul Mitchell, without whom the exhibition would not have been possible in its present form. His work dovetailed with the contribution by architect Herbert Peter, who meticulously and impressively reconstructed the medieval synagogue.

We would also like to thank all those who contributed to the audio commentaries on individual exhibition objects and specific research questions: Mika Boros, Sigrid Czeika, Karin Fischer Ausserer, Alfred Galik, Alexandra Hylla, and Andreas Rohatsch.

Further thanks are due to the designers Gerhard Abel and Dawit Kassaw (PLANET architects) for the fruitful collaboration and their willingness to join us in reimagining our aesthetic concept of the Middle Ages. Special thanks go to Stefan Fuhrer for his tireless commitment. Apart from contributing to the overall exhibition design, he was also responsible for the graphic design of the exhibition, its publicity, and this catalogue.

Contemporary art can offer us a different view of historical events and personalities. For that reason, we invited Anna Artaker and Andrew M. Mezvinsky to create artistic installations for the exhibition. Our thanks to them for the inspiring collaboration and its impressive results.

Two cooperation partners deserve special mention: Michaela Kronberger, Head (Objects), Curatorial Department of the WIEN MUSEUM, our largest lender, for her continuous support and many stimulating conversations; and Karin Fischer Ausserer, Director of the Vienna City Archaeology Department, for her enthusiasm and support.

From the present forward into the Middle ages, from the present-day museum forward to the Judenplatz of the past: We understand the museum first and foremost as a place for discourse and discussion. For us, it is therefore not a place for dwelling on the past, but one that is firmly rooted in the present. We encourage visitors to ask critical questions and to reflect on the way we acquire knowledge. Through this experience, we can acquire and hone our tools for analyzing social contexts. From the present forward into the Middle Ages, forward to the Judenplatz of the past!

View of the Mizrachi House at Judenplatz 8, which houses Museum Judenplatz. During the Middle Ages, the Schulhof (synagogue courtyard) was located in the space between this building and the adjacent structures.

The Judenmeister Lesir from *Judenbuch der Scheffstrasse* (1389–1420), the only surviving depiction of a Jew from medieval Vienna

Vienna's Jewish Community in the Middle Ages

Anna Lidor-Osprian

The beginnings of Jewish history in Austria are often described as "vague"[1] and "speculative."[2] This is due above all to the paucity of sources for the Early Middle Ages (c. 500–1050) and to medieval historiographers, whose writings were not always in line with modern-day ideas of historical accuracy. The latter also applies to sources from the High and Late Middle Ages (c. 1050–1500), which, although more numerous, often feature one-sided accounts of Jewish life. Apart from documents, the aforementioned accounts of historical events, legal texts, and commercial records, information about the history of Jewish communities can also be obtained from Hebrew sources, including rabbinical writings, gravestones, and individual chronicles.[3] Both of these groups of sources contain indications of different areas of Jewish life and together offer a deeper insight into the (everyday) history of Jews in the Middle Ages. Archaeological findings, including recent ones, are also of particular significance here.[4]

"Jews and other merchants [...]"[5]

According to the *Chronik der 95 Herrschaften*—a fourteenth-century world chronicle written by an unknown author focusing on the (sometimes freely invented) history of Austria—the Jewish history of

Austria began 859 years after the Flood. It relates that Abraham of Temonaria fled from his homeland and, because the surroundings pleased him so well, settled in a town that was later to be called Stockerau.[6] He and his descendants subsequently extended their domain to Vienna.[7] Unfortunately, this somewhat mythical part of the chronicle is not plausible, as its intention of endowing Austria and its rulers with a tradition dating back to biblical times is all too evident. Equally, the famous Raffelstetten Customs Regulations (*Inquisitio de theloneis Raffelstettensis*) from the early tenth century, although an authentic source, cannot be regarded as proof of Jewish life in Austria at that time. The regulations order both Jewish and Christian merchants to pay levies for goods and slaves. This merely proves that Jewish merchants were actively involved in the Danube trade.[8]

"There was a man in the land of Austria by the name of R. Schlomo [...]"[9]

The first documented mention of a Jew who, at least for some of his life, lived permanently in Austria and Vienna occurs in the written records of the abbey in Formbach in connection with a legal dispute over a vineyard. His name is Schlom and he was the mint master of the Austrian Duke Leopold V.[10] It was during his period of office, shortly before 1200, that the English king Richard the Lionheart was held hostage by the Babenbergs, and part of the ransom for his release demanded by the Holy Roman Emperor Henry VI was paid. It is thought that Schlom was summoned to Vienna after the arrival of the ransom.[11] A Hebrew source reports on Schlom's death, which is connected with Henry VI's crusade:

"One of Salomo's servants also announced himself as a crusader and stole four and twenty marks of his money. R. Salomo had him put in prison for it. The wife of the imprisoned crusader came running to the church on one of its feast days and loudly proclaimed that her husband was being held prisoner by the Jew. The crusaders in the city became very angry at this, left the church, burst into the just man's house, and beat him to death along with fifteen other Jews. When the duke heard of this, he ordered two of the ringleaders to be arrested and decapitated. He did not wish to punish more of them because they were crusaders."[12]

Five rabbis studying, *Ashkenazi Haggadah*, 1430-70

הקב״ה את אבותינו ממצרים
הרי אנו ובנינו ובני בנינו משעב
משעבדים היינו לפרעה במצ
במצרים ואפלו כלנו חכמים
כלנו נבונים כלנו זקינים כלנו
יודעים את התורה מצוה עלינו
לספר ביציאת מצרים והמספר
ביציאת מצרים הרי זה משובח
מעשה בר׳ אליעזר
ור׳ יהושע ור׳ טרפון
ור׳ אלעזר בן עזריה
ור׳ עקיבא שהיו מסבין בבני

Privilege issued by King Rudolf I for the Jewish communities in Austria on March 4, 1277, confirming the rights of Jews in Austria previously granted by Duke Frederick II on July 1, 1244

After his violent death, Schlom appears one last time in another source. According to a document from 1204, he seems to have owned four properties in the present-day Seitenstettengasse in Vienna. Next to these sites, the document says, there was also a "judenschul," the first synagogue in Vienna.[13]

"[…] took place in the house of the Jew Teka"[14]

It is not until many years later that a further Jew, Teka, is mentioned by name in Vienna. He too was a high official, serving the Hungarian king Andrew II. Teka owned property in the Duchy of Austria and had a house near or in Vienna.[15] It is unclear whether he lived in Vienna or Austria for a long time. Presumably it is also this Teka who appears as a robber knight in a literary collection of letters.[16]

Privileges and establishment

Thirteenth-century sovereign privileges provide evidence of the formation of a permanent and growing community in Vienna. Privileges are generally documents listing and confirming various rights and obligations of groups or individuals. Along with more detailed collections of secular or religious rights, they formed the legal basis for the existence of a Jewish community in a particular territory or town. The first privileges for the Viennese Jewish community contained rules for business transactions (e.g. interest rates) as well as regulations serving to protect life and limb, personal property, and community infrastructure (synagogues, cemeteries, etc.).[17] Emperor Frederick II issued the first privilege of this kind for the Vienna Jews in 1238; a further privilege, valid for all Jewish communities in Austria, was issued by Duke Frederick II of Austria in 1244. This "Fridericianum," as it was called, formed the basis for all future privileges awarded to Austria's Jewish communities.[18]

In return for the protection offered by the secular and religious authorities, Jewish communities had to pay them special taxes and levies. The Austrian dukes actively protected the Jews, keeping the Vienna community in particular safe from attack, and also gave shelter to Jewish refugees from other regions in times of crisis.[19] The relative security and favorable legal situation in Vienna attracted many Jews to the city in the Late Middle Ages. The names of the Jews who settled in Vienna around the thirteenth century provide an indication of their origins.[20] Teka and some other Slavic names come from Bohemia/Moravia, and also Hungary. But most of the new members of the community were probably from closer by, for example from the neighboring Duchy of Styria and other towns ruled over by the Duke of Austria.[21] It is estimated that the Vienna community around 1400 numbered about nine hundred people.[22]

"[...] to the Viennese and Rabbi Avigdor, who lives there"[23]

While Christian sources make little mention of the existence of a Jewish community in the thirteenth century, Hebrew sources give indication of its gradual establishment in Vienna. Around the middle of the thirteenth century, two important and renowned Jewish scholars lived in Vienna: Isaac ben Moses, known as Or Zarua, and Avigdor ben Elijah ha-Kohen. Isaac ben Moses was a well-traveled man, whose own writings testify to the many places of his teaching and learning. Parts of his main work, *Or Zarua* (scattered light), were written in Vienna. Or Zarua's contemporary Avigdor ben Elijah was equally eminent and had contacts with scholars all over Europe.[24] As early as the thirteenth century, he was running a yeshiva (Talmud school) in Vienna, which became highly reputed under one of his successors, Meir ben Baruch Ha-Levi.[25]

In view of the increasing persecution of Jews in Germany and their relative safety in Austria, Vienna and Wiener Neustadt in particular developed into new centers of rabbinical activity and scholarship.[26] As teachers and writers, the "Austrian" rabbis of the fourteenth and fifteenth centuries were of major importance to future generations in Ashkenaz (the usual term for Central and Eastern Europe in Hebrew sources).[27] Along with Meir ben Baruch, Abraham Klausner was another respected scholar of the time. He is also considered to be the author of a description of Austrian traditions and customs.[28] The surviving writings of Viennese rabbis and their students are important sources of information about religious, but also everyday life in the medieval Jewish quarter.

Introducing children to Torah study, *Leipzig Mahzor* (prayer book for the High Holidays and festivals), c. 1310

Kahal Wina–the community of Vienna

Within the Jewish community, there were various administrative, legal, and religious-ritual institutions and functions, which were operated by officials appointed by the community. Once a year, the community chose three representatives or spokesmen (parnassim) from its midst. Among other duties, they were responsible for collecting taxes and enacting community directives (takkanot).[29] They also managed the money in the welfare fund (tzedakah),[30] which was used to pay for the hospital and for poor relief.[31] Because of the importance of these tasks for community life, only respected, well-connected, and most likely wealthy men were chosen for this office.[32] In order to become a rabbi in a community, scholars had to be officially ordained after their studies by one of their teachers (semikah). They were mainly involved with legal affairs and arbitration on matters of religious or marital law. Most rabbis were also active in education and headed a yeshiva. They were generally unpaid, and many of them also practiced moneylending for that reason.[33] Two further community functions were connected with the synagogue: The cantor (hazan) led the prayers and service in the synagogue.[34] The sexton (shammas) was responsible for calling the men to daily prayer, but also had responsibilities outside the synagogue. He served the rabbinical court (beth din), certified documents,[35] and announced official proclamations.[36]

In addition to officials and institutions, the community infrastructure also included several buildings and facilities for living according to the religious laws (halakha). In the center of the Jewish quarter, on today's Judenplatz, was Vienna's (second) medieval synagogue. It was remodeled several times and also enlarged as the community grew.[37] The synagogue was a place not only for reading and studying the Torah, but also for hearings before the Jewish court and for public transactions and rituals.[38] It has not yet been possible to establish the exact location of the ritual bath (mikveh). Written sources indicate two possible locations, one inside and one close to the Jewish quarter. Although no archaeological evidence of the precise location of the mikveh in Vienna has been found, it is highly likely that Vienna's Jewish community had at least one such ritual bath.[39] Also of importance was the cemetery, which according to the religious rules had to be outside the Jewish quarter.

Jewish cemeteries could only be laid out on land belonging to the community or to an individual member of it, as they were intended for eternity. It is thought that, even before 1244, there was a cemetery in Vienna,[40] where other communities could also bury their dead. The "Fridericianum" not only mentions cemeteries and their protection, but also permits the transport of the dead for burial without the payment of tolls.[41] The cemetery in Vienna was outside the city walls, "Im Gereut" near Kärntnertor, although its precise location cannot be determined.[42]

The hospital (*hekdesh*), first mentioned in 1379, was next to the synagogue.[43] Like Christian hospitals at the time, it was used not only to look

Picture of a Seder celebration from the *Ashkenazi Haggadah* (1430–70). The Seder is celebrated at the start of Pesach and serves to recall and retell (haggadah) the Exodus from Egypt.

after the sick and old, but also to provide for the poor and as overnight accommodation for travelers. The cost of the hospital was covered by the aforementioned welfare fund.[44] Fourteenth-century sources also mention a kosher slaughterhouse near the Jewish quarter.[45] There are no records in Vienna of a bakery or a dance locale where festivals and marriages could be celebrated, as existed in other large medieval Jewish communities.[46]

"[...] in vigilia leonhardi werbrunnen alle judenhäuser zu wien [...]"[47]

By the end of the fourteenth and the early fifteenth centuries, the situation of Jewish communities in Austria deteriorated. The importance of Jewish merchants in economic life had dwindled, and the rulers no longer took the protection of Jews so seriously. At the same time, criticism by the Church and anti-Jewish propaganda fueled the hatred of Christians for their Jewish neighbors. Among the reasons for these changes were the precarious economic situation in the years after the Plague and the decreasing importance of Jews in commerce.[48] In 1371, all Viennese Jews were arrested and then released again, presumably on payment of a ransom.[49] Some years later (1383), Duke Albert III arrested David Steuss, head of one of the most important and probably wealthiest Jewish families in Vienna and extorted 50,000 pfund pfennig from him.[50] But it was not only the dukes who attacked the Jewish community. Viennese citizens used the pretext of a fire that broke out in the Jewish quarter on November 5, 1406,[51] to ransack Jewish property. It was only at the order of Duke Leopold IV that some of the stolen objects and property were returned.[52] This was not an isolated incident, because shortly before, on November 1, students at the University of Vienna were ordered to return stolen items to their Jewish owners.[53] Incidents like these are an indication of the politically unstable situation in the Duchy of Austria after the death of Duke William in the summer of 1406 and also clearly demonstrate that the safety of the Jewish communities could not be guaranteed without an economically strong ruler in Austria.

Column fragments, possibly part of the parapet of the bimah (podium from which the Torah is read), found among the remains of the destroyed synagogue on Judenplatz during the archaeological excavations in the 1990s

The excavations on Judenplatz, 1996: the future site of the display room has already been fully excavated, and archaeological features have been protected against the elements. Work is continuing in front of the Mizrachi House at Judenplatz 8.

Judenplatz and the Former Jewish Quarter

Archaeology and building research since 1995

Paul Mitchell

Between July 1995 and November 1998, a major excavation took place on Judenplatz for an overall period of twenty-one months with lengthy interruptions.[1] In the western part of the square, where the Shoah Monument stands today, over 600 square meters were thoroughly investigated, and in the east, around the Lessing monument, a similar area was documented to a lesser depth. The excavation was pioneering, not because of its size, but on account of the quality of the documentation, with a total of 6,542 context numbers (layer, wall, and trench numbers) recorded,[2] 637 hand drawings prepared, and over 100,000 artifacts from two millennia recovered. In the middle of the site, the ruins of the synagogue destroyed in 1420/21 were uncovered and its entire former extent recorded.

The synagogue and its surroundings

The type of construction, accompanying pottery finds, and a coin no older than 1236 found in the mortar of the oldest floor suggest that the synagogue was built around 1240–50. It was sited at the rear of what may have been two narrow plots, whose front was on the present-day Wipplingerstrasse. In the initial building phase, the synagogue—like the young community at the time—was not very big. The core building covered an area of just 12 × 9.4 m, and the entire structure was about 17.5 m wide.

The bimah (the podium from which the Torah is read) just after it was unearthed in 1995

Excavations near the Schulhof (synagogue courtyard), 1996

The men's shul, the main room in the synagogue reserved for men, faced southeast and was flanked by two annexes. An entry passage was identified in the north, presumably the entrance for the men, which means that the women's shul would have been to the south.

In a second phase, dated at around 1280 on the basis of a historical source from 1294 and comparisons with similar buildings, a much larger, Gothic structure was built. The men's shul was extended to a length of around 18.4 m. The imposing two-aisled space with two columns and a

The remains of the bimah in the archaeological display room of Museum Judenplatz

vaulted ceiling supported by buttresses reflects the growth in size of the Jewish community, which by now was one of the largest north of the Alps. The circular base of the new bimah (the podium from which the Torah is read) in the center of the men's shul has survived, although it was soon replaced, possibly in the early fourteenth century, by a hexagonal bimah typical of southern central Europe. Its tiled floor and the post-hole for the lectern have survived. Only fragments remain of the steps and floor in front of the ark from this and other phases.

In the fourteenth century, the Jewish community must have grown further, as the synagogue reached its maximum size of over 460 square meters during that period. A double vestibule with an area of 90 square meters was added to the west of the old building. The men's shul was entered through a new archivolted portal. In the eastern part of the building, narrow courtyards were built over, thereby extending all three of the rooms. Remains of benches made of stone and brick were found in all annexes. In the men's shul, women's shul, and north room, which, after the modifications to the building, now had only one entrance and was therefore possibly used as a winter synagogue or yeshiva (schoolroom), the floors were covered with green, yellow, and red-brown glazed tiles.

To the west of the synagogue was the initially small shul yard, which by 1294 had grown large enough to border the present-day Mizrachi House (Judenplatz 8) and thus occupied an area of around 300 square meters (approx. 20 × 15 m). It was surfaced on several occasions with crushed stone and rubble, including stonemason's waste, and at its center, at least until around 1300, was a storage pit. Since the southern end of the yard was enclosed by a wall with no opening, it must have been entered through a narrow passage along the north side of the synagogue. The yard was bordered to the south and northwest by houses, but to the northeast by the hospital, which served as a hostel, clinic, and welfare center for the community. Today, only a single corner of this building remains. The mikveh (ritual bath) was probably situated not right next to the yard but just to the north of the synagogue. A record from 1425 mentions a "tukhaus" (*Tauchhaus* or immersion bath) in the southern part of the present-day Wipplingerstrasse 11.

To the south and east of the synagogue complex were streets that were often repaired. A street running north to south connected the present-day Futterergasse and Parisergasse and was once part of a 300-meter route through the city (from the Danube escarpment to the Graben). On the southwest side of the synagogue was a short street leading to the present-day Drahtgasse. On both streets opposite the synagogue were houses, in the east a large building around today's Lessing monument, with many rooms on the ground floor and two basement rooms. A private well from the late fourteenth century (not before 1386, according to dendrochronological investigations)[3] and the site of an oven or fireplace were uncovered.

Investigation of the Mizrachi House

After the decision was made to incorporate the Mizrachi House (Judenplatz 8) into the project as an access route to the underground

Work being carried out in 1999 inside the Mizrachi House at Judenplatz 8: a workman is removing Baroque vaulting; a spiral staircase is visible in the background, leading from the ground floor to the first floor.

display and on-site museum, an investigation of the building was carried out to discover more about its history.[4] From 1996, the two-level basement from the sixteenth and seventeenth centuries was documented in a degree of detail hitherto unseen in Austria. Later, when construction commenced and the building above the ground floor was gutted, the investigation was gradually extended to the entire building. Standardized documentation was devised for all historical phases, and plans were drawn up of all floors, using color-coding to mark the masonry from different periods. Furthermore, archaeological excavations were carried out in the courtyard and basement.

Seating niches from the late thirteenth century in the entrance to Parisergasse 1, 2020

The Altes Rathaus on present-day Wipplingerstrasse with the basement of a fourteenth-century Jewish house, 2020

It emerged that the core of the Mizrachi House consisted of solid rubble masonry dating from the late thirteenth century. At that time, this site, together with the eastern section of today's Wipplingerstrasse 15, was part of a large plot of over 800 square meters belonging to a Jew called Pendit. The shul courtyard was bordered by the short side of a large L-shaped structure of at least 10 m in height (two upper floors), but without a basement. In terms of today's façade, it occupied the two window axes on the left up to the top edge of the first floor. In the past, it would have had a gabled or hipped roof. After the destruction of the Jewish quarter, the building was modified and enlarged several times. Most of the current structure dates back to the second quarter of the sixteenth century and the period around 1694.

Extension of the research

The excavations on Judenplatz and the detailed investigation of the Mizrachi House marked the start of an intensive examination of the remainder of the medieval Jewish quarter, which lasted around ten years.[5] No construction work was undertaken without archaeological accompaniment. The first results were presented even before the opening of the museum: an intact basement room in Färbergasse 6; a basement with a central column and brick vaulting underneath Jordangasse, not far from Wipplingerstrasse; a side-gabled building on Drahtgasse (no. 3); and two structures and three wells in the basements of Kurrentgasse 6–8.

After the monument and synagogue project had been completed, work continued from 2000 until 2002 in the buildings at Schulhof 2 (intact basement room) and Parisergasse 1 (an extended building with seating niches, a large well, and four slit windows), and in the Altes Rathaus (parts of several medieval houses, including a fully preserved single-column semi-basement room from the fourteenth century and a small cellar underneath Wipplingerstrasse). In the basement of the building at Am Hof 13, remnants of a tower and other fragments were documented that were formerly part of the Babenberg palace. The protective presence of the duke's palace, situated here until the 1270s, may have been the primary reason for the settlement of Jews in this particular area. The foundations of two gates to the Jewish quarter were uncovered in Färbergasse (1998) and Parisergasse (2001).

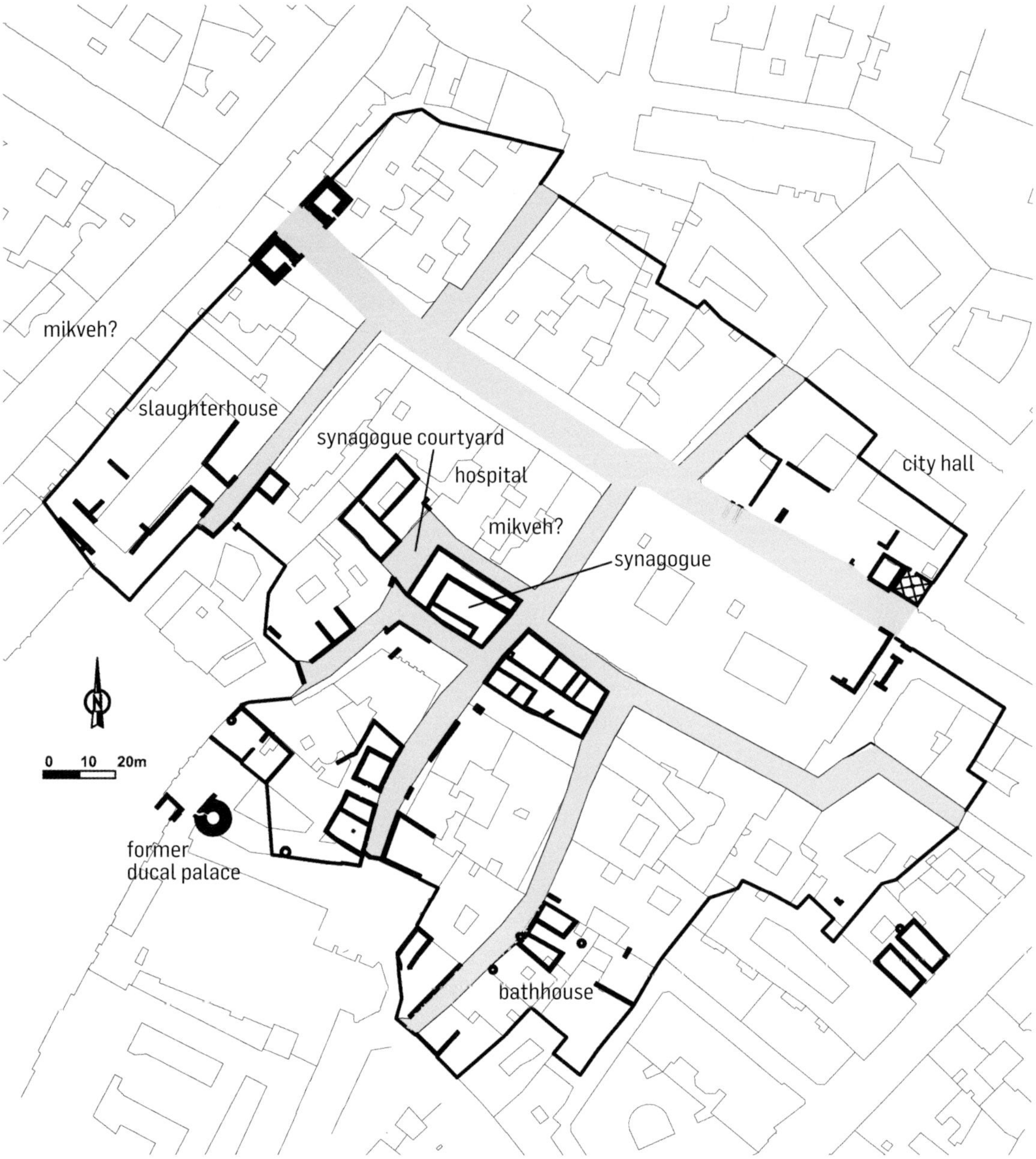

This map, drawn by Paul Mitchell in 2020, shows the present situation on and around Judenplatz. The remains of the medieval Jewish quarter revealed by the archaeological investigations are marked in black.

After 2002, new findings emerged in the buildings Am Hof 12 and Schulhof 6, both of which have a medieval core. In the northeast wall of Am Hof 12, a small, bricked-up window from the fourteenth century was discovered at the first-floor level and has been restored. It is now visible from Drahtgasse. In 2005, remains of the community slaughterhouse and a neighboring building were found in the basement of the Bürgerliches Zeughaus (Am Hof 10). The slaughterhouse had a six-meter-wide entrance drive and a large inner courtyard. Following an investigation of the cellar walls, archaeological excavations revealed remnants of a building at the back of the courtyard.

Construction work in this part of the city center tapered off after 2010, and with it archaeological excavations also slowed down. Nevertheless, some medieval masonry has recently been uncovered in the building Kleeblattgasse 7.

Jewish houses looked no different from Christian ones. They were made of stone and had one or two upper stories and sometimes also basement rooms. The ground floor was used for work and storage, and the upper story was the living area. In the courtyard stood outhouses, sometimes half-timbered. The former Jewish quarter contains some of the finest examples of medieval residential architecture still in existence in Vienna today, including the most graceful seating niches (Parisergasse 1) and one of the most attractive basement rooms (in the Altes Rathaus).

Topography of the Jewish quarter

On the basis of the projects discussed above and the current situation, the following conclusions may be drawn about the layout of the Jewish quarter. The area developed gradually from the early thirteenth century onward.[6] It was to the west of the commercial center of medieval Vienna, around Hoher Markt, and was traversed by a street running southeast to northwest, today's Wipplingerstrasse. Not far from this street, on the northeastern boundary of the quarter, was the early fourteenth-century town hall, remnants of which still survive. After the gate on Hohe Brücke, originally the *porta principalis sinistra* of the Roman fort, the street crossed Tiefer Graben, thought to have been the site of an early fourteenth-century mikveh known by the name of "Wunderburch"[7] (Tiefer Graben 19). In addition to two shorter lanes, now Drahtgasse and Kurrentgasse, the quarter was accessed via two southwest/northeast axes. On the first of these, following the line Parisergasse–Futterergasse–Stoss im Himmel, about halfway along on the western side, was the synagogue. The second axis, along Färbergasse and Schwertgasse, connected the Babenberg palace (Am Hof) with the church Maria am Gestade. On the left, directly after the southwestern gate to the quarter, was the entrance to the slaughterhouse. Six gates in total have been identified, either

through archaeological investigations or from pictorial sources. The streets in the quarter were surfaced with gravel or rubble. Sewage channels made from wood, brick, or stone were discovered at Judenplatz and Am Hof 10.

At the heart of the Jewish quarter was the synagogue with the shul courtyard behind it to the west, which could be reached only by a detour from the main thoroughfares. On the shul courtyard was also the hospital, and in the space between the hospital and the synagogue was another, probably more recent, mikveh.

During the fourteenth century, the boundaries of the Jewish quarter shifted further to the southwest and southeast. There was a Jewish-owned bathhouse on today's Kleeblattgasse (no. 5). In the east of the quarter (around Jordangasse 5 and 7) was a complex belonging to the Steuss family, including what is described in the records as a "Cantorey" (possibly a synagogue or yeshiva). David Steuss attempted unsuccessfully to extend the complex as far as today's Tuchlauben (nos. 17 and 19).

The events of 1420/21 brought about abrupt and radical changes in the quarter. The Jewish inhabitants were murdered or expelled; a small number of them were forced to convert. The duke sold or gave away their houses. The slaughterhouse became a timber yard and, later, the city arsenal. The synagogue and building opposite to the east were demolished and a new square laid out in their place. The pit left by the razed synagogue was filled in with rubble and food waste. Only the name Judenplatz kept the memory of the community alive.

It seems that the archaeological investigations of the former Jewish quarter have now passed their apex. There are still interesting buildings and areas that could be examined further, but future analysis will no doubt concentrate on scientific (archaeological, historical, art-historical, museological) research and appraisal of the accumulated data and findings.

Left: Fragments of a lamp found in the remains of the destroyed synagogue and among the medieval cobblestones in the street next to it during the archaeological excavations on Judenplatz in the 1990s. The lamp is thought to have formed part of the synagogue lighting. Right: Fragment of a crocket capital, possibly decorating one of the two pillars.

Following double page: Judenplatz in 2020 with the Lessing monument, the Memorial to the Austrian Jewish Victims of the Shoah, and Museum Judenplatz in the background on the right.

LA PERLA

MUSEUM
JUDENPLATZ
ZAHNARZT

Judenplatz 8: A Jewish House with a Varied History

The first written source mentioning the site of the present-day Museum Judenplatz dates from 1294 and indicates the owner as "Pendit, the Jew."[1] Jewish owners are documented until 1420/21: Merchlein in 1373, and Rötel from Klosterneuburg in 1379 and again from 1381 to 1420/21. Following the Vienna Gesera of 1420/21, Duke Albert V confiscated this and other buildings in the Jewish quarter and gave or sold them to individuals he wished to reward for political or religious reasons. Around seventy houses were acquired by Christians in this way.[2] Over the centuries, Judenplatz 8 was occupied by merchants and burghers, until it was acquired in 1694 by a member of the aristocracy, the Duchess of Zeyhl. In 1860, it was purchased by Riunione Adriatica di Sicurità, an insurance company, which sold it two years later to Anna Mandeles, the first Jewish owner since 1421. The Mandeles Foundation owned the house until it was assigned by ministerial decree in 1939 to the General Foundation for Jewish Welfare established by the Nazis. In 1950, it was restituted to the Vienna Jewish Community (IKG), which in 1971 gave it to the Vereinigung Thoratreue Zionisten der Misrachi und des Hapoel Hamisrachi, Landesverband Österreich. Today, Judenplatz 8 is a place that unites Jewish past, present, and future. Apart from the museum, it also houses a synagogue and a Zionist youth club.

Astrid Peterle

Removal of floor slabs as part of the refurbishment of the building at Judenplatz 8, 1999/2000

Façade of Judenplatz 8, 2020

This tile with a depiction of Venus dating from the second half of the seventeenth century, along with many other stove tiles, was found in the basement of Judenplatz 8 during the archaeological investigation of the building between 1996 and 2000. It was among the material used to fill in the stairwell abandoned during the Baroque era.

VENUS

Map of Vienna by Jacob Hoefnagel, 1609, with detail showing Judenplatz; visible in the lower right-hand corner is the recess in the street frontage, indicating the site of the medieval Schulhof (synagogue courtyard).

Jewish-Christian Cohabitation in Medieval Vienna*

Eveline Brugger / Birgit Wiedl

The legal basis that governed the lives of Jews in medieval Vienna was complex. Papal law fluctuated between protection (such as the ban on forced baptism) and separation of the Christian and Jewish communities (for example, through prescriptive clothing), even if the latter was largely ineffective in practice.

Ducal legislation had a more direct influence. In 1244, the last Babenberg, Frederick II, granted a privilege to the Jews that was to form the legal basis in Austria for the remainder of the Middle Ages. Apart from strict protection provisions, it included above all rules for moneylending and surety, making clear the duke's economic interest in his Jewish subjects, who were considered part of his *Kammer*, i.e. his treasury. The privilege also introduced the office of the *Judenrichter* (judge of the Jews), held by a Christian member of the urban elite, to adjudicate in legal disputes between Jews and Christians.[1]

There was also a rabbinical court confined to internal Jewish matters[2] and the numerous local, usually municipal regulations, which applied to both Jewish and Christian inhabitants. Thus, not only did legal disputes arise for a wide variety of reasons, they were also settled by a number of different courts. Everyday disputes were usually adjudicated by local courts (*Schrannen-, Grund-* and *Berggerichte*), particularly in cases involving real property and the associated levies. The procedure

before Viennese courts was the same, whether it was the Jew Tenichel, who in 1372 (successfully) sued a Viennese burgher regarding a viticultural and advocatus levy (*Berg- und Vogtrechtsabgabe*), or the Saint Clare nunnery in Vienna, which a few years later (also successfully) sued Tenichel's widow for outstanding *Burgrecht* (special privilege) payments.[3]

Jews and Christians met at a variety of social levels. The Jewish community itself was not a homogeneous group, but structured in a hierarchy of economic and social categories. The sources refer mostly to the higher social classes, as these groups kept written records. Until the mid-fourteenth century, it is therefore primarily the relationship between the Jewish and Christian elites that is documented. A mutual influence regarding tastes and lifestyle is evident at least at the highest social level.[4]

Elements such as clothing, jewelry, and tableware were seen and used by both sides as status symbols; interior furnishings and wall paintings not only reveal similar aesthetic tastes, but also show the familiarity of Jews with popular literary motifs.[5]

This leads to the question of which language was used in everyday Jewish-Christian interaction. In many cases, Christian scribes were probably employed by Jewish merchants to record German-language documents, but for personal negotiations and everyday affairs, communication with the non-Jewish populace in the local language was not only necessary for survival but also a matter of course. In comments written in Hebrew on commercial documents, clearly intended for use within the Jewish community, there are German words written in Hebrew letters and traces of German syntax and grammar. Moreover, the form of the rare official documents written in Hebrew closely followed the structure of German-language documents.[6] It may be assumed that German was the everyday language of the medieval Jewish community.

Although moneylending had become the most important economic activity of the Jewish population—and was explicitly encouraged by the duke—it was not the only profession Jews were allowed to practice. For their own infrastructure—synagogue, slaughterhouse, and ritual baths, for example—large communities like Vienna required community employees, such as synagogue attendants and butchers, who would also

Fragment of a medieval drinking vessel and a jug found among the remains of the synagogue during the archaeological excavations in the 1990s. These everyday items are not specifically Jewish but indicative of a shared material culture in the Middle Ages.

provide services to Christian neighbors and business associates if required. The synagogue attendant, for example, was called upon by Christians who wished to address the Jewish community as a whole or individual members "from the outside" in order to inform them of the decisions of a Christian court or to summon them to appear before one.[7] Although the religious authorities on both sides were inclined in theory to keep the two population groups separate,[8] even a large community like the one in Vienna could not have existed in complete segregation, as it was reliant on the services of Christian artisans and servants.

The synagogue and surrounding houses formed the Jewish quarter, satisfying the requirement for the Shabbat enclosure or eruv. But it was by no means a ghetto. Jews were allowed to inhabit or own houses outside the Jewish quarter, and the boundaries were primarily ritual markings for the benefit of members of the community rather than a demarcation for Christians, who continued to inhabit the adjacent area and enter the Jewish quarter. While the inside of the synagogue may be regarded as an exclusively Jewish space, its forecourt was defined in 1244 as an official court venue for disputes involving Jews—but was also used for other official or business announcements by Christians.[9]

So, what were the interpersonal relations like? It can be assumed that Jews and Christians entered each other's houses. Jewish merchants entered Christian homes to do business, and Christian customers entered the homes of Jewish moneylenders or sent Christian messengers.

Jews could own property both inside and outside the Jewish quarter. For that reason, neighborhood disputes between Jews and

Recent archaeological investigations on the present-day Kleeblattgasse near Judenplatz (shown here in a photo from 2016) revealed masonry from the time of the medieval Jewish quarter.

Christians in the tightly packed medieval city were just as common as disputes between Christian neighbors—and all parties had the same legal recourse. Building alterations that allowed Jewish neighbors to see into exclusively Christian spaces could have a religious component, although similar disputes also arose between Christian neighbors. Jews also objected, for example, to having to look at the cross of a nearby church: Rabbinical commentaries frequently stipulated that houses built near churches should avoid windows with a direct

Document about the legal dispute between Jakob Poll and Merchlein, Vienna, August 23, 1373

view of the church—or that existing windows should be bricked up.[10] Such concerns were handled pragmatically by the municipal court, even in cases where Jewish and church properties overlapped. For example, in 1373, Jakob Poll, chaplain of the Vienna Rathauskapelle, took his Jewish neighbor Merchlein to court because Merchlein had built an unauthorized kitchen in his courtyard, from which smoke and unpleasant odors entered Jakob's house, wafting as far as the chapel. It would have been easy to give this case a religious spin, but this did not happen. The religious aspect of a Jew allegedly defiling a Christian religious space was not even mentioned in the hearing, even if the sideswipe by the plaintiff about the "impure smell" from the kitchen might have been hinting at the anti-Jewish stereotype of the "Jewish stench", the *foetor judaicus*. The city councilmen treated the dispute as a routine matter and sent two council members to investigate, as was customary in such cases. Merchlein was ultimately ordered to remove the unauthorized kitchen and to raise the chimney higher so that smoke and odors could no longer permeate Jakob's house or the chapel.[11]

In many comparable cases, the matter in dispute was more prosaic, such as the construction of a latrine in the backyard, which the Jew Hessmann shared with a building owned by the Teutonic Order. The construction was approved, albeit with detailed conditions, by the municipal court. In fact, latrines, wastewater, and the associated smells were a frequent cause of neighborhood disputes—whether or not these involved Jews.

The fact that municipal court judgments were notable above all for their pragmatism and, like debt, purchase, and sales documents, were free of anti-Jewish sentiments should not conceal the fact that anti-Jewish sentiments were always present among the city's inhabitants: "daz die verfluchten juden vil pezzer recht habent gegen den christen denn die christen gegen den juden" ("that the accursed Jews have much stronger rights against Christians than Christians against Jews"), complained the author of the Vienna city law book, a private compilation of municipal ordinances, written before 1360.[12] In contrast to other Austrian cities, the Jews in Vienna remained safe from open persecution for a long time. In 1338, when the repercussions of the alleged host desecration in Pulkau went far beyond Austria into Bohemia and

Dice and game tokens found among infill rubble southwest of the synagogue and in the Schulhof (synagogue courtyard) during the archaeological excavations on Judenplatz in the 1990s. Dice games were a popular pastime in medieval Vienna. Even though frowned upon by both religions, historical sources indicate that Jews and Christians alike engaged enthusiastically in these games and that the two groups even played together.

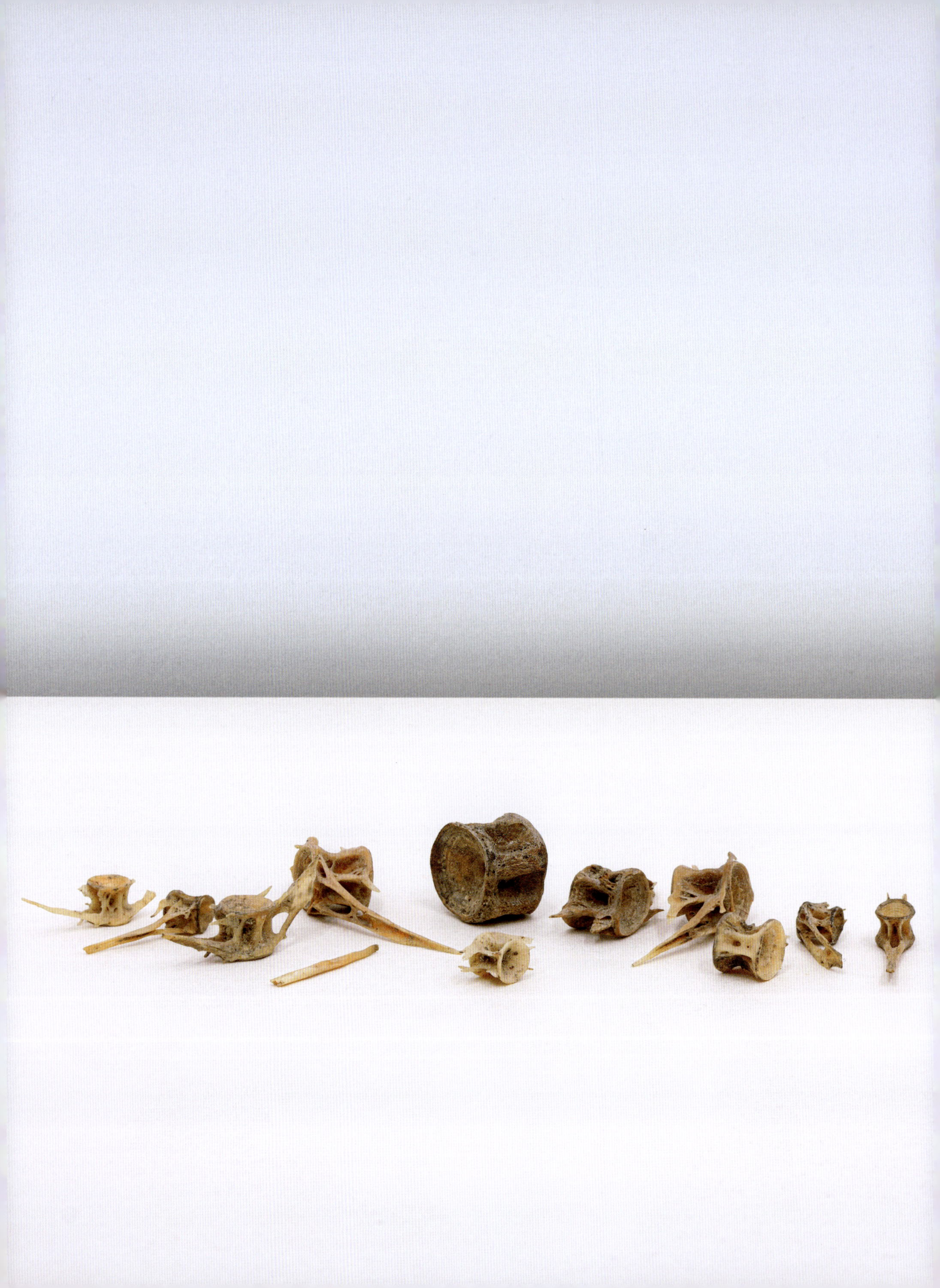

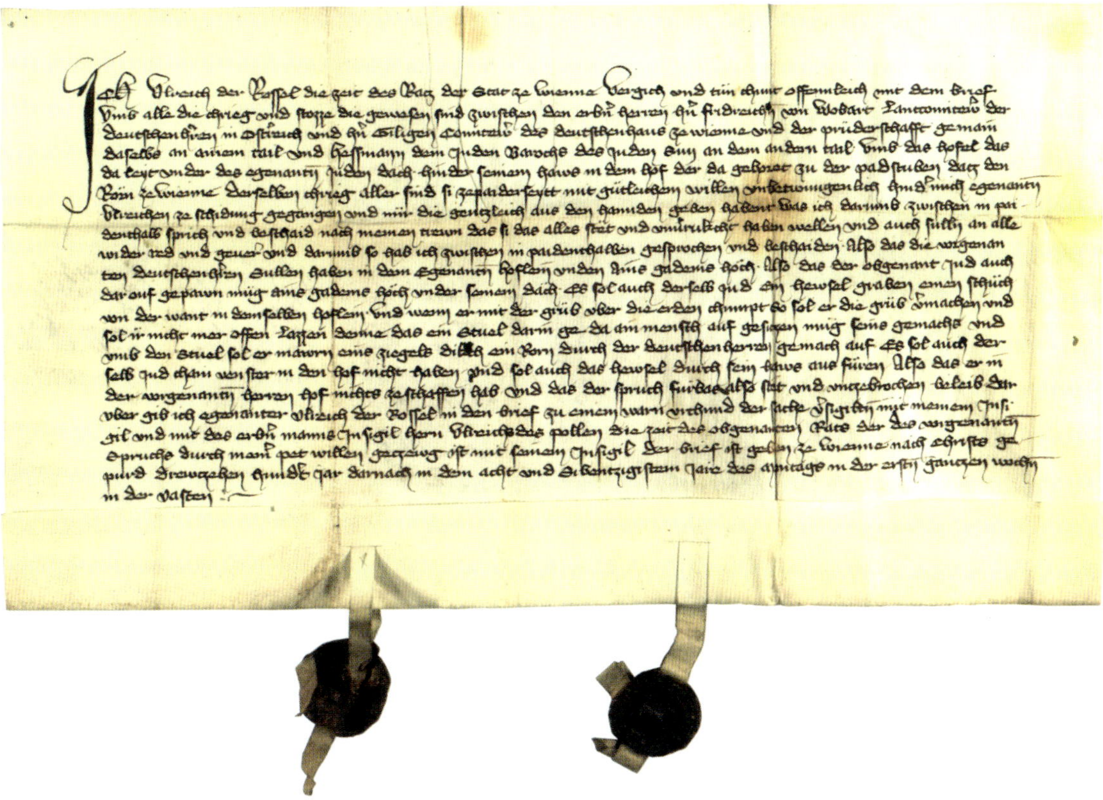

Court verdict on the dispute regarding modifications to the house belonging to the Jew Hessmann, Vienna, March 8, 1378

Moravia, the Viennese community was spared, albeit at the price of considerable economic concessions to the citizens of Vienna. When persecution raged through the empire ten years later during the period of the Plague, the firm intervention of Duke Albert II also protected the Viennese Jewish community from violent attacks.[13]

The second half of the fourteenth century, however, brought a change in the Habsburgs' attitude toward the Jews. The protective approach of the thirteenth and early fourteenth centuries gave way to a view of the Jewish population purely as a source of ducal revenue, even if, until the early fifteenth century—in other words, until shortly before the Gesera—the dukes still made sure not to completely ruin the Jewish moneylenders so as not to deprive themselves of revenues from the Jewish levy.

The citizens of Vienna were only peripherally involved in the Vienna Gesera initiated by Duke Albert V, but this did not prevent them from profiting from the murder and expulsion of their Jewish neighbors when the duke redistributed the houses stolen from the Jews.[14]

Fish bones, including those of whiting, pike, and carp, give clues about the diet of the Jewish quarter's inhabitants. The bones were found in 2008 during an archaeological excavation at Am Hof 10 and were preserved between layers of excrement in a medieval sewage channel. These fish are not necessarily characteristic of Jewish cuisine, but rather refer to the typical diet of the time.

Mysterious Tokens: Coin-Like Lead Objects from the Synagogue Courtyard

During the archaeological excavations on Judenplatz in the 1990s, lead objects dating from 1250 to 1400 were found at the level of the synagogue courtyard. They are round, flat, and show a variety of motifs: eagles, stags, dogs, flowers, and a royal couple. These symbols are not specifically Jewish, but were commonplace in medieval Christian painting, architectural sculpture, and on coins. Because of their similarity to coins, they were initially thought to be tokens for payment within the community or in certain stores. However, there are no other records of token money made of lead being used in medieval Austria. The fact that most of these lead disks were embossed only on one side and that they were much larger and heavier than normal coins, suggests that they may have been used as playing tokens for games such as backgammon, checkers, or nine men's morris, which were already popular in the Middle Ages. Or they could have served as play money or as a calculating aid, especially as they were found in the synagogue courtyard, which also served as the schoolyard. In fact, relatively inexpensive handmade tokens like these could have been used for all kinds of purposes, and their actual use is hard to determine with certainty. It is also unclear whether the objects belonged together as a set. One piece, however, revealed its purpose just recently. It consists of two round disks pressed together and joined by a tab, thus forming a lead seal used to mark goods, such as fabrics, on which duty has been paid.

Mika Boros / Alexandra Hylla

Following double page: Medieval coins from the twelfth to fifteenth centuries found during the archaeological excavations on Judenplatz in the second half of the 1990s

Lead tokens and a lead seal from between 1250 and 1400 found during the archaeological excavations on Judenplatz in the second half of the 1990s

א
רוב נסים הפלאת

Hansüß, Rifka, Joseppin: Women in the Medieval Jewish Quarter

Martha Keil

Introduction–about the three names

Hansüß, Rifka, and Joseppin may be strange-sounding names, but each one gives a small insight into medieval life in the Ashkenazic (German-speaking) Jewish communities. Without even knowing anything more about the women concerned, their three names already offer some cultural and historical clues. The name Hansüß has two components: the first comes from the biblical name Chana (Hannah, from the Hebrew *chen*, meaning "compassion," "grace"), wife of Elkanah and mother of the prophet Shmuel (Samuel). Her eloquent prayer in praise of God can be found in the Bible (1 Samuel 2:2–10). The second component, *süß*, meaning "sweet," is a typical attribute added to southern German Jewish names. The names of both men and women would be given these endearing, childlike suffixes, as well as the diminutive forms *-el*, *-lein*, or *-chen*. The nickname Süßel or Süßlein could be given to boys (also as Süßkind or Süßmann) and girls alike.[1] These were given names or nicknames in everyday use, continuing into adult life and work. For all religious contexts, however, such as the writing of names in a marriage certificate (ketubah), divorce document (get), and on a gravestone, and for men when they were called up to read the Torah or for other purposes in the synagogue, the *shem hakodesh*—the holy, usually Hebrew, name—was used.[2]

Women with books, depicted in the *Darmstadt Haggadah*, c. 1430

The *Krems Ketubah* (marriage contract), 1391/92, is the oldest example in the German-speaking world of a marriage certificate with figurative depictions. In the fifteenth century, it was cut into four pieces to be used in the binding of a collection of manuscripts, a codex by the theologian Thomas Ebendorfer. After the expulsion of the Jewish community in 1420/21, many Hebrew manuscripts suffered a similar fate. Except for the cut-out middle sections, the *Krems Ketubah* has survived in full.

Rifka, by contrast, is a clear biblical name, taken directly from the Torah (Genesis 24–27). As the wife of Yitzhak (Isaac) and the mother of Jacob, Rifka (also Rivka, often transcribed as Rebecca) is one of the four matriarchs of Judaism and, according to the Jewish interpretation, as the mother of Esau, also of Christianity. Our third representative, Joseppin, acquired her name from her husband Josef. The feminized form of masculine given names, later also surnames and professions, was common in both Christian and Jewish society. Confusion can occur above all with professions. Was "Bakula die sankmaisterin" in Vienna the wife of the hazan, the cantor who leads the prayers, or was she one of the rare (in medieval times) female cantors for the women's section in the synagogue? The name alone does not tell us which is the case.[3] Joseppin's actual name was Sarah, or Serlein, and she was the wife—and from summer 1375 the widow—of Josef of Feldsberg (Valtice), as well as one of the most active female moneylenders in Vienna.[4]

Visibility

Behind these prototypical names are three women from the Jewish upper class, who are mentioned in records on account of the prominence of their families or husbands and their successful business activities. In historical research, however, they did not become visible until historians began to take a greater research interest in women. In older Austrian-Jewish historiography women are not mentioned, or, if at all, only as the wives of famous or important men. Independent references to them in source material were overlooked or ignored, or—as also occurred in some instances—interpreted as referring to men.[5] Emerging in the USA in the early 1970s, the discipline of women's studies and, arising from this,

Seal of Dislaba, a Jewish woman from Regensburg, 1391

gender studies, began to ask questions about the agency of women in legal and social contexts, leading to a more balanced depiction of historical societies. It took another two decades, however, before this gendered approach found its way into German-speaking Jewish studies.

In 1993, the Israeli economic historian Michael Toch stated that on average roughly a quarter of loans in forty-one Jewish communities listed in the encyclopedia *Germania Judaica* were given by women.[6] Using their ketubah, widows would often continue their husbands' businesses, alone or with their sons, sons-in-law, and sometimes also their daughters. The situation in Jewish communities in medieval Austria was highly diversified. Where small or medium-sized loans to local artisans or less wealthy citizens were concerned, Jewish women were very active. This is clearly evident in a unique and highly informative source, the *Judenbuch von der Scheffstrasse*,[7] which covers the southeastern area outside Vienna up to Stubentor and to the west of the Wien River (now in the 3rd district), listing not only land registers and Christian loans, but also Jewish loans for the years 1372 to 1420. Around one-third of the loans were granted by women, including the three women mentioned in the title of this essay. Between 1390 and 1399, Joseppin von Feldsberg conducted thirty transactions, either alone or with her seven sons, sons-in-law, or grandsons. By comparison, the highest number of transactions by a man, a David "von Drauberg," who does not appear elsewhere in the records, was thirty-eight. Rifka, the widow of Rabbi Abraham Klausner (died around 1408), granted at least thirteen loans, either by herself or with her son Schaul. Hansüß, daughter of David Steuss, the most famous moneylender of the time, is listed with only one transaction. In view of her father's prominence, she took on his name rather than that of her equally important husband, Rabbi Meir ben Baruch ha-Levi of Erfurt or Fulda.[8] Röslein of Tyrnau (now Trnava, Slovakia), not mentioned as a moneylender in other sources, is listed with eight transactions. Gaya, "Chnoflachin"—Knoblauch (garlic) was a common name both among Christians and Jews—is listed with seven transactions, together with her son and son-in-law, as is Hannah, the widow of Peltlein of Salzburg.[9] Her loan of a modest seven pounds to Niklas Prüder and his wife Elsbeth on March 10, 1420, with two presumably equally modest houses as surety, is the last entry in the *Judenbuch*. From May 1420, the Jews of Vienna began to be imprisoned by order of Albert V. It may be assumed that Hannah was one of the prisoners, possibly after having already escaped the terrible burning of Jewish men and women in Salzburg sixteen years earlier.[10] At all events, she was still in Vienna in August 1420. Her daughter Lea was forcibly baptized and by way of reward received a house under her new name Elspeth die Newkristinn ("the new Christian"). The fate of Hannah's second daughter Schöndl is not known.[11]

Success in business

Although it was relatively rare for women in Austria to transact large loans—compared with the large Jewish communities in Germany, such as Frankfurt, Regensburg, or Koblenz[12]—the sources nevertheless contain some notable women moneylenders. The first Jewish woman mentioned in Austrian records, Dreslinna—from the Slavic name Drazna or Drasna meaning "graceful"—received 100 pounds of Viennese coins from none less than the Austrian state scribe Konrad of Tulln for a pledged vineyard.[13] This is her only mention, however. There are much more frequent references to Plume (Plueme) of Klosterneuburg, the matriarch of an entire dynasty of bankers and rabbis. She is thought to have arrived around 1320 from Regensburg, settling deliberately outside but still near enough to Vienna, in Klosterneuburg, from where she built up her business. Her son-in-law Hendlein—one of three known sons-in-law—took her name, and not, as was customary, his father's, as did her sons Rötlein and Häschlein.[14] Thus, she was not only a successful businesswoman, but also the mother of at least five children. Apart from several loans to Viennese burghers, usually with vineyards as surety, she lent the impressive sum of 800 pounds of Viennese pfennigs to the counts Eberhard and Heinrich of Wallsee-Drosendorf, a transaction in which even the Duke of Austria Albert II was involved.[15] From April 1359, her grandson David Steuss is mentioned. Although he is sometimes named after his father Hendlein, he often appears under the name of his far more prominent grandmother, who laid the foundations for his career as the most successful banker in medieval Austria. David Steuss's daughter Hansüß also followed in Plume's footsteps. She granted mostly small and medium-sized loans, either on her own or together with her husband Rabbi Meir ben Baruch ha-Levi of Erfurt or Fulda, her stepson Salman, various other male names, probably relatives of hers, or with her fellow-rebbetzin (wife of a rabbi)

Rifka. There is only one record of a larger loan of 200 pounds—to Thomas, the abbot of the Schottenstift (Scottish monastery) in Vienna.[16]

The most successful businesswoman in medieval Austria, however, was Sarah, called Gutlein, of Wiener Neustadt. She too continued her husband's business after his death. For years, she led her sons-in-law in their struggle to recover an outstanding loan of 6,812 gulden from Count Jörg of Pottendorf, inherited by her and her heirs from her husband, Isserlein, son of Merchlein, for which the market community Kirchschlag and all of its seigneurial rights had stood as surety. Whether she was ever able to recover this large sum or whether, as a woman and a Jew, she was able to draw revenue from this unusual surety is unfortunately not recorded.[17]

Summary and gaps in our knowledge

The documents give an insight into the transactions, customers, and also the social status and networks of these women, but they offer few clues about their education or their everyday, religious, and social life. Apart from their origins, marital status, and assets, the symbolic capital of these women can be indirectly inferred: reading and probably often writing, arithmetic skills, linguistic expression, social bearing, and self-confidence.[18] In some cases, we know the number of children. On average, there were two or three sons and, although less frequently mentioned, a similar number of daughters who survived to adult age. Exceptionally, the parnass (community leader) of Vienna and top banker Lebman—his Hebrew name was Marlevi ha-Kohen—for whom records exist for the years 1295 to 1314, and his wife Weichsel (Wyschna) are documented with the impressive number of six sons and five daughters.[19]

The interest from the loans also produced considerable tax revenues, which were of vital importance for the community and hence brought these women taxpayers a certain amount of recognition. Furthermore, wealthy women were able to become involved in the synagogue through religious endowments and donations to charity, even if they were excluded from the main room, which was for men only. Although, beyond these documents, there is no other reliable material evidence about Jewish women in medieval Vienna, their significance can also be inferred from the "women's shul" annex to the synagogue, references in rabbinical literature, and not least their presence in municipal administrative records.

The restored mural from the house at Brunngasse 8 in Zurich, which was owned in the 1330s by a prominent female Jewish moneylender by the name of Minna. The mural was discovered in 1996 and is thought to have been part of the décor of the room where customers were received. The Hebrew inscriptions in the coats of arms suggest a Jewish owner.

Following double page: Women's shul in the synagogue, Museum Judenplatz archaeological display room, 2020

Who Wrote Manuscripts in the Middle Ages? Hannah bat Menahem: An Example of a Female Scribe

Not all manuscripts surviving from the Middle Ages have an identifiable named writer, and there is even less evidence of female scribes. We know very little about Jewish women scribes in the Middle Ages. One of the few to be identified by name is Hannah, daughter of Menahem Zion, who lived in the second half of the fourteenth century, probably in Cologne. She copied the Sefer Mitzvot Katan (Small Book of Commandments), written originally by Joseph of Corbeil in the thirteenth century. We know that Hannah was a scribe from her own note in the colophon on the last sheet of her book, a page with details of the scribe, place, and year, where she writes:

"I, Hannah, daughter of [R.] Menahem Zion, completed this book on the eleventh day of the month of Tammuz in the year 146 of the sixth millennium [June 10, 1386]. May God lead his people to freedom and protect them from worry and need. And may He hurry to give them succor. Amen. Quickly."[1]

Most medieval books, be they of Jewish or non-Jewish origin and content, were written anonymously. Even if we assume that female scribes were an exception in the Middle Ages, some of the manuscripts currently understood to have been produced by male scribes could well have been written by women.

Anna Lidor-Osprian

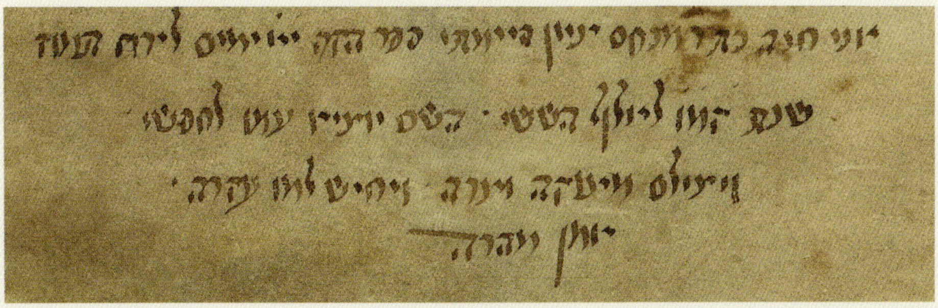

Signature of the female scribe Hannah bat Menahem, 1386

Ceramic jug (aquamanile) in the form of a Jew, with the pointed hat typically attributed to Jews in the late Middle Ages, found in Krems an der Donau, first half of the fourteenth century

May the Impure Serve to Clean

A late medieval jug in the form of a Jew, found in Krems an der Donau

Thomas Kühtreiber

In the course of history, humans have invented an incredible number of things to facilitate their life as biologically "deficient beings." There is also evidence, from the earliest times, of symbolic interpretations of objects and their use, particularly in a religious context. This in turn resulted in special versions of "everyday items" that reflect such ritual components. They often differ from commonplace items through the use of higher-quality materials, more elaborate craftsmanship, or a specific form. The distinction between a common and a ritual object can also be blurred, as in pre-modern cultures the secular and religious aspects of life overlapped and were not seen or experienced as separate spheres. The study of the relationships between humans and objects, also known as "material culture," can offer insights into the interactions between function and meaning of objects in earlier times.

The fragmentary 17 cm ceramic jug in the form of a hybrid creature with an animal body and a human head, to be found at the museumkrems, offers such an insight.[1] While the body is only roughly sculpted, the artist paid more attention to the head. The chin, nose, and mouth are finely modeled in clay, and two clay rings are set into the eye sockets as eyes. The eyebrows are formed by two curved lines of punctured holes. On the back of the head, a similar row of stamped holes on a narrow bulge below vertical grooves indicates a head of hair with a roll curl in the neck. This hairstyle recalls the "Manesse style," named for the illustrations in the *Codex Manesse*, a book of songs and poetry from the first half of the fourteenth century.

The figure is wearing a pointed hat, clearly identifying him as a Jew depicted in the medieval pictorial tradition.[2] The fact that this figure is a household object can be deduced from the tubular spout protruding from the front of the body, held in stylized hands. The back, of which only fragments remain, has the vestiges of a handle, but no trace of an opening for filling the vessel, which would presumably also have been there.

Vessels in the form of figures have been known in the Middle East and Mediterranean region since Neolithic times and were probably used until pre-Christian antiquity for wine, particularly at ritual feasts.[3] A direct formal connection can be made between these objects and cast metal objects in the form of animals in the Persian and Islamic empires of the Early and High Middle Ages, although the few museum items that have survived do not offer much insight into their purpose.[4] Similar figurative objects were made from the twelfth century onward in Central and Western Europe, with metal, particularly bronze or brass, being the preferred materials until the thirteenth century. The repertoire extended from horseback riders to animals such as doves, cockerels, and deer, and mythological figures such as dragons, basilisks, centaurs, or sirens.[5] From the mid-thirteenth century, figurative ceramic vessels are

Bible illustration showing Jews with pointed hats, typical of central European depictions of Jews since the twelfth century, 1250–1300

also documented, particularly in southern Germany, Switzerland, and Austria,[6] as well as brass or ceramic jugs with spouts in the form of animal heads.[7]

All of these medieval vessels are connected with hand-washing rituals in the tradition of ancient feast rites, but have also been documented since late antiquity in the context of the Christian mass.[8] Although there was no standard term for these vessels in the Middle Ages, the jugs with animal-head spout are generally referred to as "lavabos,"[9] while "aquamanile" is the customary term for vessels in the shape of figures.[10] "Lavabo" refers to Psalm 26:6 "I wash my hands in innocence, and go about your altar, Lord," which according to the Torah refers to the cleansing ritual for Jewish priests before serving at the altar.[11] Aquamanile is a compound word made up of *aqua* (Latin for "water") and *manus* (Latin for "hand"), thus referring explicitly to hand-washing.[12] Both terms are therefore closely connected with a religious or ritual context, even if traditions had changed considerably from the Jewish congregation in the tabernacle in Mosaic times to the medieval Christian religious service.[13] By contrast, there are few contemporary written or pictorial sources explicitly referring to the use of vessels for ritual hand-washing in private homes, as can be inferred from medieval texts about courtly dining culture.[14] An exception here are Hebrew inscriptions on aquamanilia, evidently added to the objects later and offering a clear indication that these vessels, which come from a Christian context, were also used by Jews.[15] A lion aquamanile, for example, now at The Walters Art Museum in Baltimore, has an inscription in Hebrew: "Blessed are you, O Lord, our God, King of the Universe, who has sanctified us through your commandments and has commanded us concerning the washing of hands."[16] This blessing is said as a morning prayer and, according to the Babylonian Talmud, was to be spoken since the Middle Ages after washing hands and before breaking bread at the start of a meal.[17]

As to the design of the figures on aquamanilia, the general consensus in recent research is that all creatures can be interpreted as personifications of virtues and vices. Written records, particularly about Christian animal symbolism, building on antique writings such as *Historia naturalis* by Pliny the Elder, contain abundant and often contradictory

Dragon aquamanile, bronze with red glass eyes, Lower Saxony, early thirteenth century interpretations regarding the representation of good and evil. In connection with the element of water, however, it is possible to identify the properties that were likely to have determined the motifs on pouring vessels. It is interesting to note that allegories of vices clearly predominate over those of virtues.[18] To date, these interpretations have been based solely on metal aquamanilia, however. Because of their simpler form, ceramic vessels have not been given the same attention. Apart from riders and a few centaurs, the dominant creatures in the six hundred or so surviving ceramic objects are rams, dogs, and pigs. This predominance is also found among the animal-shaped spouts of lavabos, with the addition of rabbits. These same animals occur in another seemingly unconnected context, namely in medieval interreligious polemics. Christians, Jews, and Muslims alike used these animals as a demeaning way of denoting other religious groups. Specifically, the moral-ethical impurity attributed to these animals, in particular their lack of sexual restraint and greedy eating habits, was emphasized and projected onto other religions.[19]

The Christian association of Jews with lust (*luxuria*) is evident in a dragon aquamanile, now in the Museum für Kunst und Gewerbe Hamburg. Clasped in the dragon's jaws—the ultimate symbol of evil—is a monk, representing the endangered Christian soul, while four naked creatures are clambering on the dragon's body, one of which is a monkey eating fruit (gluttony), another is a Jew with a pointed hat. This figure is holding his member in an obscene manner, which can plausibly be seen as an allegory for lust.[20]

In a similar vein, the spout of the Krems ceramic aquamanile, held with both hands by the Jewish figure, could also be seen as an allusion to an erect penis, again making this figure a personification of lust from a medieval Christian perspective. The association of the Jew with corrupt morals can also be seen in a further detail: The imprints on the neck roll imitate the impression of a cloven hoof. It can be assumed that this implied suggestion of a goat's foot—and hence the devil—is intentional.

So, why were Jews and animals represented as ethically and morally impure creatures on medieval hand-washing vessels—that is, on objects that were used for ritual cleansing? This very much reflects the dialectic thinking of the Middle Ages, in which the negative and evil also had its place in the history of salvation. Just as "the Jew" was necessary in medieval theology so that Jesus could perform his redemptive work, human vice is shown as an incentive to betterment. The hand-washing ritual was a means not only of acknowledging a person's own sin, but also, through the symbolic re-enactment of the priestly hand-washing, of guiding a person toward a virtuous life. All creatures—and hence also pouring vessels in the form of animals or humans—thus place themselves in the service of God's salvific mission.

Back of the jug (aquamanile) in the form of a Jew, with the pointed hat typically attributed to Jews in the late Middle Ages, found in Krems an der Donau, first half of the fourteenth century

Gravestones: Relics, Building Material, Trophies

Jewish gravestones are among the most important relics of Jewish material culture. Ideally, Jewish cemeteries and the gravestones in them should last forever–hence the Hebrew word for cemetery: *bet olam* (house of eternity). However, the historical reality of expulsions and destruction suffered by Jewish communities meant that this ideal condition has rarely ever been achieved. When a community was expelled, its cemetery was usually appropriated by the ruler. The gravestones, although by rights the property of the deceased, were used as valuable building material, while the site was sooner or later built over. The use of gravestones as building material was a common practice. In the process, the gravestones were often crushed or cut to size and thereby destroyed. However, Jewish gravestones were also sometimes visibly incorporated into churches or prominent buildings. This use–which may be seen as political in the widest sense–was like a public display of the triumph of Christianity over the ostracized Jewish religion: gravestones as prize trophies. Traces of their use in buildings now bear witness to this practice. For example, gravestones from the medieval Jewish cemetery near Kärntnertor were used in the foundations of the Hofburg chapel in Vienna, which was itself built as a symbol of the triumph of the Church over the Synagogue.

Domagoj Akrap

Hebrew inscription on the gravestone of a young man called Aharon bar Baruch, who died, possibly of bubonic plague, in 1349

אמן סלה

Five medieval Jewish gravestones on the western city wall near Schubertweg in Wiener Neustadt. The photograph dates from 1939/40 and was taken by the teacher Reinhold Graf, who, out of personal interest, took many photos of Wiener Neustadt around that time.

This fourteenth-century gravestone is immured in the outer wall of the Maria Schnee Carmelite Convent in Graz. The inscription is so weatherworn that only a few letters are readable today. However, a translation by Rabbi David Herzog from Graz in 1936, when the inscription was more legible, has survived: "Abraham, son / [of] Samuel / [who left us] in sorrow [in] 1343/44."

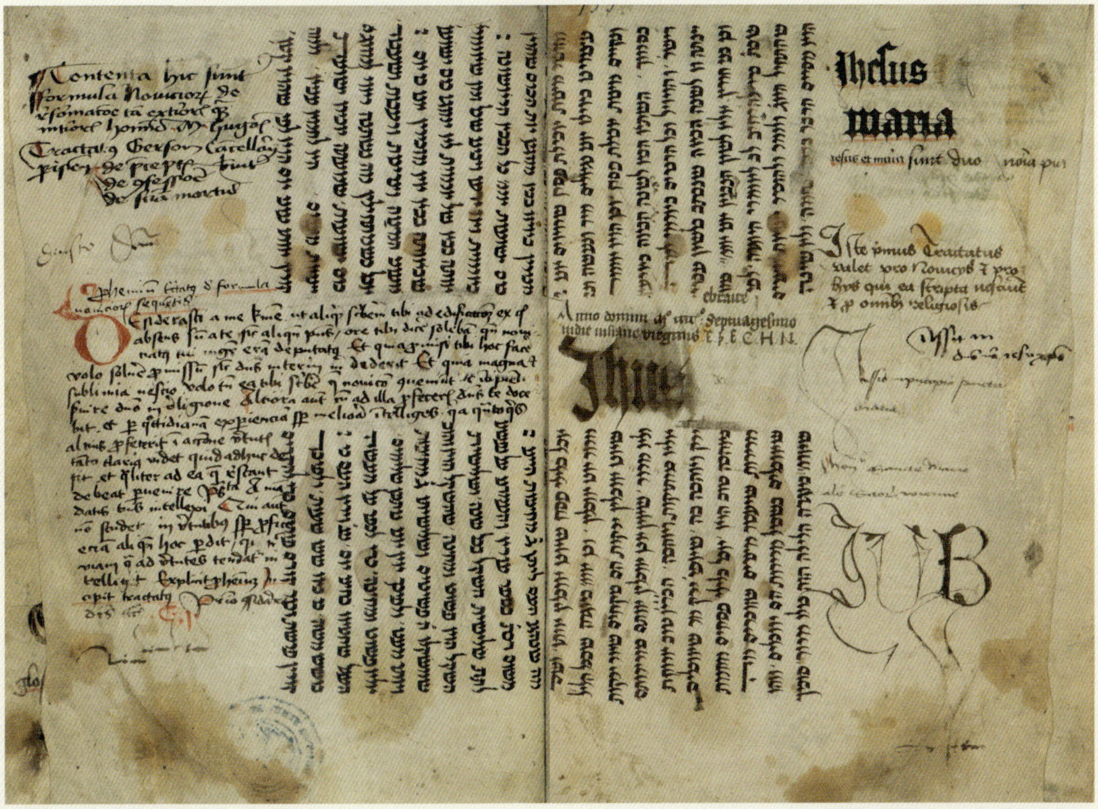

Hebrew fragments in a Christian book, probably dating from the thirteenth century. Because of their material value, it was commonplace in the Middle Ages to use Hebrew manuscripts in the binding or as endsheets in Christian codices (manuscript collections). For Jews this represents a defilement, because Jewish law stipulates that religious books must be buried when they are no longer used.

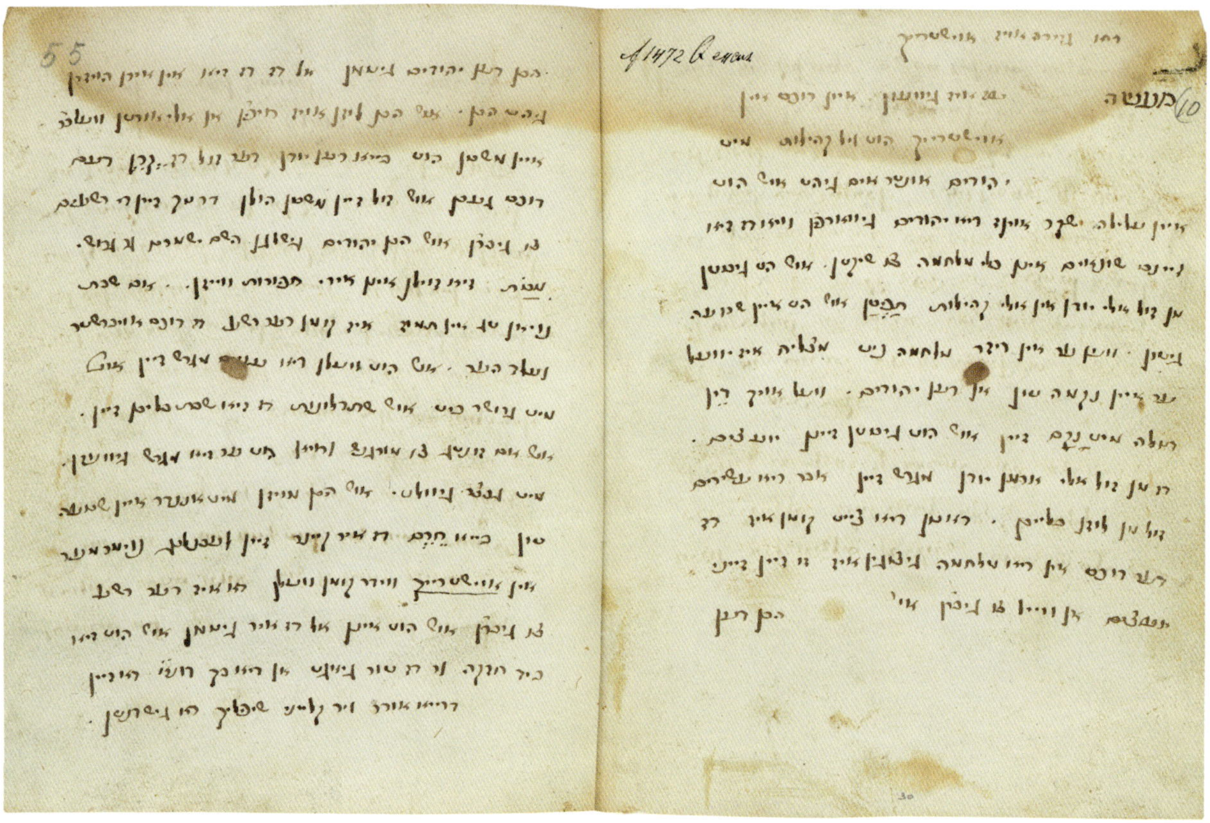

The initial pages of "Di gezeroh oiz Oistreikh," a report written in Yiddish using the Hebrew alphabet about the Vienna Gesera, manuscript, second half of the sixteenth century

Q&A on the Vienna Gesera

Four perspectives on the history of the expropriation, expulsion, and murder of the Viennese Jewish community in 1420/21

1

How do you explain the Vienna Gesera to someone who has never heard of it?

Martha Keil The Hebrew verb *ligsor* originally means "to cut," but it is also used in the sense of "to decide" or "to judge." Since the Middle Ages, the word *gesera* has come to be interpreted as a negative decision, an anti-Jewish law, and, ultimately, a disaster and persecution.

Klaus Lohrmann The Vienna Gesera is the name given to the expulsion and persecution of Jews from present-day Upper and Lower Austria (with the exception of Wiener Neustadt/Neunkirchen) that took place between the spring of 1420 and March 12, 1421. The name "Gesera" comes from the title of a work recounting the disaster from a Jewish point of view in order to preserve the memory of the devout martyrs. The decisive events took place in Vienna. The Hebrew word *gĕzerāh* means "judgment" or "decree"; one translation also speaks of an order by a non-Jewish ruler.

Simon Neuberg For someone like myself who is mainly involved with language and the written word, the *Wine'r ge'sèro* is a complex of four texts—reports on the atrocities of the pogrom against the Jews of Austria in 1421. These reports also represent important historical sources and are a classic example of the processing of such tragic events: in an attempt to document them in a meaningful way, events are embellished with fantastical elements and perceived by survivors and their descendants as the story of their deliverance.

Petr Elbel / Wolfram Ziegler The Vienna Gesera is a pogrom that took place under Duke Albert V of Austria in 1420/21, leading to the expulsion and murder of the Austrian Jews. The sources clearly show that it was planned and carried out by the ruling authorities. It started with the duke's order to round up and imprison the Jews in the cities governed by local rulers (May 1420). Jews without means were then expelled to Hungary, while the wealthier ones were tortured to extract cash and securities from them. Led by clerics associated with the University of Vienna and the monastery in Melk, an attempt was made to forcibly baptize the captured Jews as a pseudo-legitimizing byproduct of the pogrom. Most of the Jews refused to be baptized, however, and some of the Viennese Jews chose to commit suicide in the synagogue. After even the Pope spoke up against the forced baptisms, the duke ordered the remaining Jews to be executed on March 12, 1421, on the pretext of alleged host desecration.

2

What is so unique about the Vienna Gesera in the history of medieval Jewry in German-speaking countries?

Martha Keil Expulsion, persecution, and pogroms are a common thread throughout centuries of medieval Jewish history. Most of them, however, were not an "eruption of spontaneous public anger" but rather events orchestrated by the authorities. Accusations of well poisoning, host desecration, and ritual murder were the usual reasons for violence against Jews, sometimes even culminating in Jews being burned at the stake. In the case of the Vienna Gesera, however, the accusation of collaboration with the Hussite enemy—even within the framework of medieval legislation—should have been punished by expulsion. The burning of at least 210 men and women was only retrospectively justified through the additional accusation of host desecration, said to have taken place some years earlier but, curiously, not prosecuted at the time. A judicial murder as brutal as the Vienna Gesera is unusual even for the Middle Ages.

Klaus Lohrmann The Vienna Gesera was a terrible and bloody pogrom that cost the lives of many Jews and deprived the survivors of their rights, forcing them to leave. A new approach to research would be required, however, to determine how unique it was in the context of historical developments in the period from 1350 to 1450. The persecutions at the time of the Black Death in the mid-fourteenth century also deprived Jews of their rights and often ended in the murder of the victims.

Simon Neuberg Still looking at the tradition of this group of texts, what makes them so unique is that we first come across them in Yiddish. Such reports are typically conceived as additions to the liturgy—for the commemoration of a specific disaster—and as such would normally always be written in Hebrew. In our case we have three texts in Yiddish, while the fourth, the only one in Hebrew that we know of, has clearly been translated from Yiddish. This is a very unusual constellation. Although it is likely that all of these Yiddish texts were based on a single lost Hebrew text, this earlier source must have disappeared a very long time ago if, already in the sixteenth century, a Hebrew text had to be reconstructed from the Yiddish version.

These documents not only give us information about the facts laid out in them, they also provide an insight into the history of dealing with disasters and of remembering places that have been lost in a tragic event. After the quasi-liturgical use of a Hebrew text, which is read out on the anniversary of the event, it is then translated orally into the vernacular, and later printed in Yiddish to be read at will. This development may have had to do with the fact that in this case the families who felt the *Wine'r ge'sèro* to be part of their history were widely dispersed and therefore unable to commemorate the event together in the same place.

Petr Elbel / Wolfram Ziegler The persecution of Jewish communities is a recurrently observed phenomenon in the Middle Ages. The frequency and intensity varied considerably, however. The pogroms centered initially on individual towns rather than entire regions or territories. This changed in the thirteenth century and culminated in a wave of persecutions in the plague years (1348–1351). Prior to this, an incident of alleged host desecration in Pulkau (1338) had already given rise to an increase in pogroms in Lower Austria and South Moravia. Later, in the fifteenth century, pogroms were predominantly aimed at the expulsion and extermination of entire Jewish communities, either in individual cities or even in entire countries. Within the context of these expulsions, initiated by the ruling authorities in the fifteenth century, the Vienna Gesera was the most comprehensive and the most violent.

3

What, in your view, was Albert V's reason for attacking the Austrian Jews?

Martha Keil In contrast to the prevailing assumption that Albert V was driven by financial motives—robbery and murder, so to speak—I believe that a religious motivation is more plausible, also because you don't kill the goose that lays the golden egg. Albert V was a very religious man who waged war unsuccessfully against the Hussites and also had some of their adherents burned at the stake. Contrary to theological interpretations, he saw Jews as "heretics," which implies that he already regarded them as "Christians" in some way. This argument is substantiated by the fact that Albert V supported, cultivated, and promoted the careers of baptized Jews to the best of his ability.

Klaus Lohrmann The historical sources point to Duke Albert V as the originator of the persecution, which poses the question as to what prompted him to do so. As early as June 10, 1419, the "topical" issue of the Hussites and their connection with the Jews was being discussed at the university. This impetus for the persecution of the Jews further compounded the aggressive attitude toward Hussites and Jews fueled by the general calls for reform at the time. There appears to be no direct connection, however, with the forced baptism of Jews in Austria, which began on May 23, 1420, by order of Albert V. For decades, rulers had increasingly been ignoring the exemption from forced baptism accorded to Jews as part of their privileges. Albert's regular discussions with representatives from the theological faculty suggest that they had exerted an influence on him. The subsequent attempts to extort money from the Jews, after Albert's unsuccessful first campaign against the Hussites, are now also thought—with good reason—to have been planned from the outset. Experts are in agreement regarding Albert's reasons for ordering the surviving Jews to be burned at the stake on the Gänseweide, a former execution site in what is now Vienna's 3rd district. The accusation of host desecration was a later legitimation for the brutal treatment of the Jews.

Simon Neuberg I will leave it to historians to consider the reasons that combined to cause such an event. What was the role of the Christian belief that burning Jews (and also heretics and witches) would give off an "aroma pleasing to the Lord"; and to what extent was it an attempt to meet an urgent financial need by means of a single mass expropriation—even at the expense of destroying a long-term source of revenue? However, this could not have been about one single ruler alone; the prevailing mood also needs to have been conducive to ensure enough willing helpers.

Petr Elbel / Wolfram Ziegler Duke Albert V had been allied politically since 1411 with Sigismund of Luxembourg, king of Germany, Hungary, and, from 1419, also king of Bohemia. In 1411, Albert agreed to marry Sigismund's daughter and heir, Elisabeth. The marriage contract was renegotiated in 1419, opening the prospect for Albert to succeed his father-in-law in these kingdoms, which indeed occurred in 1438. The costs for these endeavors were enormous. In addition, Albert had to agree to accompany Sigismund on the Hussite crusades. The first of these crusades was announced in March 1420, shortly before the arrest of the Austrian Jews by Albert's officials. This points toward Albert's motivation, as he was in financial straits caused by his participation in the crusade and also because of anticipated payments for the marriage. Whether the duke really did accuse the Austrian Jews of supplying the Hussites with weapons in 1420, as one sixteenth-century source claims, cannot be verified with certainty. The death sentence Albert pronounced on the Jews makes no mention of it. The main focus was the confiscation of Jewish assets to enable Albert to pursue his political objectives—paying Emperor Sigismund for the marriage and adding considerable amounts to the ducal treasury, which still showed a substantial surplus in the years 1423 to 1425.

4

What research still needs to be done on the Vienna Gesera and what results would you like to see?

Martha Keil Of course, it would be very useful if the lost accounting books and lists of Jewish property confiscated before the Gesera were to be found, so that the financial aspects could be clarified. But this is likely to remain the wishful thinking of a historian. One thing that is absolutely necessary is a critical and, if possible, interdisciplinary new edition of the *viner gsere*, the early sixteenth century Yiddish text relating the brutal events in the form of an eyewitness report by a survivor. It might, hopefully, provide insights about an original version, possibly in Hebrew, text variants, the influence of older sources, as well as the date and place where it was written, and perhaps even indications of the authorship or at least the context in which it was written. The *Pohrlitzer Memorbuch* listing the Vienna Gesera martyrs, re-published in 1928 and even then existing in fragmentary form only, could also be re-examined. It should at least be determined whether any of the fragments still survive today.

Klaus Lohrmann In the course of a more detailed interrogation of the historical records on the Austrian Jews, we can expect further additions and clarifications regarding the chronology of events. Precise and considered comparisons with other persecutions of the time need to be carried out, because at present we have only passing reference to attacks on Jews in other places, which have not been studied in greater detail. Further theological research could also be useful, but only if it is carefully aligned with older research. All of these tasks can be addressed satisfactorily only if a new critical analysis of the Vienna Gesera becomes available.

Simon Neuberg From my perspective, there is an urgent need for a critical edition that places the four text versions side by side as a basis for all further research. With any luck, however, we will not have to wait too long for this.

Petr Elbel / Wolfram Ziegler In the first place, there is a need for a new edition and critical analysis of the various versions of the Jewish *Wiener Gesera*, all of them early modern texts, which contains numerous early modern Jewish historiographical themes. Further, it is not known where exactly the expelled Jews were able to settle. We know only of Hungary and Styria. Moravia, South Bohemia, and Bavaria would also be likely candidates. Details of the duke's financial gains also require closer scrutiny. We know of the enormous increase in revenue during the years in question from summary lists of the duke's revenues and expenditures. Further study is required, however, of other relevant historical sources, in particular regarding the land and property outside Vienna that was seized. This would give a better understanding of the course of events and the fate of the Austrian Jewish communities, and of the groups of individuals who benefited from the pogrom besides the duke.

Wise Stones Falling into a Sea of Doubt An installation about the 1420/21 Vienna Gesera by Andrew M. Mezvinsky

Stones from the synagogue destroyed in 1421 were used to build the university in Vienna on today's Bäckerstrasse. It was not by accident that stones from the house of prayer and Jewish scholarship were used for this new building. The university record of December 22, 1421, contains a statement in Latin that translates as: "The synagogue of the Ancient Law is being wondrously transformed into a school for teaching the doctrine of salvation of the New Law."

To mark the 650th anniversary of the University of Vienna in 2015, the Jewish Museum Vienna organized an exhibition entitled *The University: A Battleground*, for which the Vienna-based US American artist Andrew M. Mezvinsky created a video installation exploring the Vienna Gesera of 1421.

The work, on display at Museum Judenplatz since 2017, has been modified and extended for the new permanent exhibition. It now also addresses the fact that, apart from stones from the synagogue, Jewish gravestones were incorporated into churches and other buildings as a triumphant anti-Jewish symbol of Christian supremacy.

Mezvinsky elaborates a dense narrative based on the Albertinian Map of 1421/22, the oldest map of Vienna (now in the WIEN MUSEUM). He locates the synagogue in the city and then visualizes its brutal destruction. Viewers are given a vivid impression of the obliteration of the first Jewish community in Vienna.

Adina Seeger

Video stills from Andrew M. Mezvinsky's installation *Wise Stones Falling into a Sea of Doubt*, 2015/2020

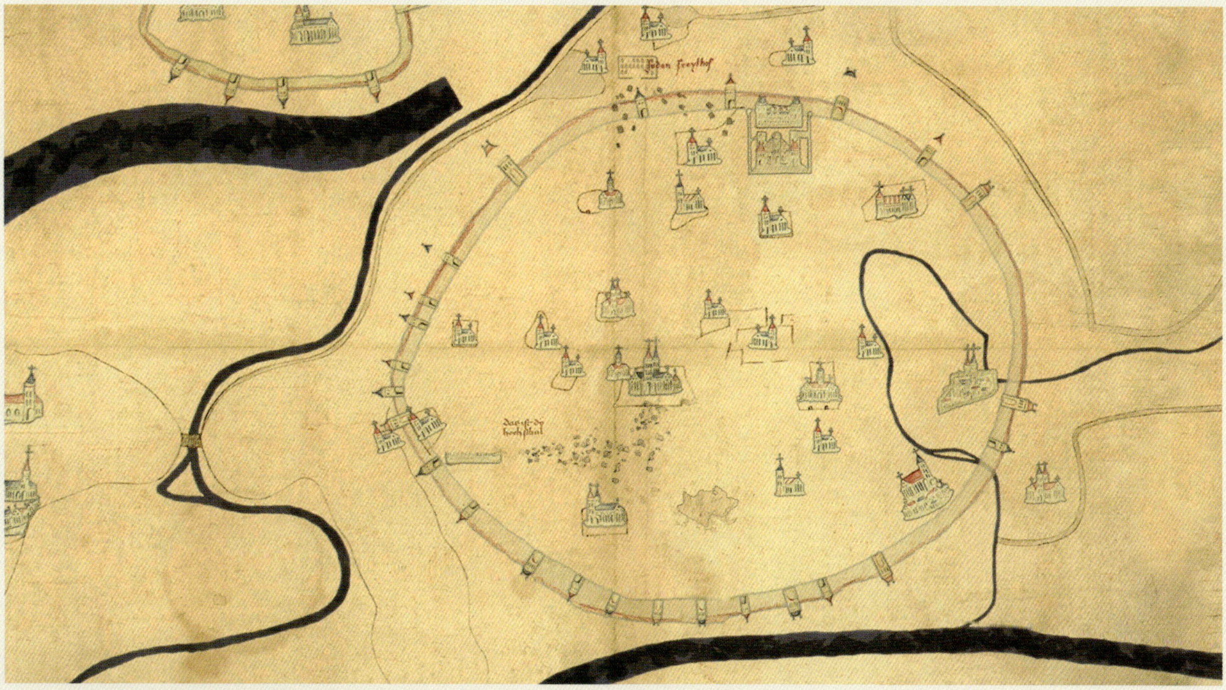
Juden Freythof

1421, 22. Dezember der Universitätsversammlung legte der Universitäts Su-
perintendent Magister Johannes Angel vor, dass der Magister Lubann
(fürstlicher Minister) die abgebrochenen Steine der Synagoge der Juden für
ein neues Gebäude der Universität bestimmt habe, falls die Universität
auf eigene Kosten dorthin beför
diese Steine.
Synagoge - Judenplatz 1421 n. Chr

Depiction of Jews in a document listing tax payments by the Jewish community of Norwich, England, c. 1233. This illustration directly associates Jews with both money and the devil: a devil figure points at the Jews' noses to emphasize them as a typical feature.

Anti-Jewish Stereotypes from the Middle Ages until Today

Nora Berend

The extent to which modern antisemitism is a continuation of medieval ideas about Jews has been debated, especially since the Second World War.[1] Some emphasize the major qualitative difference between the Nazi policy of mass murder and earlier anti-Jewish actions, even including pogroms, which never amounted to a state policy of methodically killing all Jews. Such a position resembles the self-critical stance initiated by Salo W. Baron, who objected to the "lachrymose conception" of Jewish history, the over-emphasis on Jewish suffering and the envisioning of Jewish history as a series of persecutions; more recently, similar criticism has been leveled at the narrative of victimhood.[2] Focus on the particularity of modern antisemitism can also be coupled to a distinction between anti-Judaism and antisemitism. The former supposedly targets only the Jewish religion, labeled as inferior or objectionable; hence, changing religious affiliation allows full integration into society for converts to Christianity. The latter frames antagonism as a matter of supposed race, thus leaving no route to a change of identification and integration. The distinction ultimately harks back to the late-nineteenth-century invention of the term antisemitism, and the new, supposedly scientific biological understanding of difference. While the distinction anti-Judaism / antisemitism can sometimes be fruitful, such a neat division is misleading: for example, from the twelfth century, suspicion of Jewish converts, and even of the descendants of converts, was expressed. In the Iberian Peninsula, with the introduction of *limpieza de sangre* statutes from the middle of the fifteenth century, new Christians were assigned a permanently inferior position compared to old Christians. Moreover, distinguishing physical features were ascribed to Jews in medieval art already from the late twelfth century. Therefore, it is not necessarily so easy to separate attitudes against Judaism from attitudes against Jews; nor is it an entirely modern practice to assign Jewish identity to those who do not espouse it.

Indeed, scholars have expressed diverse opinions on the exact relationship between anti-Judaism and antisemitism. Some restrict the use of the latter term to modern phenomena, in particular political ideology since the late nineteenth century.[3] Others apply the term "antisemitism" to all attitudes based on hatred against Jews as a group, branded as inferior or evil, and trace the history of antisemitism from antiquity.[4] The justifications of enmity vary, from cultural difference through theology to economic competition; there have been attempts to distinguish between religious, political, secular, and racial antisemitisms. Yet other scholars argue for the emergence of antisemitism during the Middle Ages and distinguish it from anti-Judaism either by its irrational psychological basis or its racial claims. According to Gavin Langmuir, when people labeled as Jews are "feared as symbols of subhumanity and hated for threatening characteristics they do not in fact possess," one can speak of antisemitism.[5] He emphasized the prevalence of "chimerical stereotypes" about imagined horrendous deeds as the turning point when anti-Judaism becomes antisemitism; these stereotypes arose in Europe from the middle of the twelfth century, and such attitudes were widespread by 1350.[6]

Yosef Yerushalmi saw the beginnings of racial antisemitism in the wake of late-fourteenth and early-fifteenth century mass conversions of Jews to Christianity in the Iberian Peninsula. *Limpieza de sangre* legislation emerged and finally gained papal and royal approval between the mid-fifteenth and mid-sixteenth century, justifying discrimination by reference to blood, branding Jewish descent.[7]

Racial thinking existed much earlier than modern "scientific" racism that developed from the eighteenth century onward; it cropped up in pre-modern religious intolerance and in xenophobia. "Scientific" proto-racial thought has also occurred since antiquity. This earlier form of racial thought focused on supposedly ingrained, unchanging characteristics, or the belief that qualities are transmitted by blood.[8] Those who do not use antisemitism as a blanket term to describe anti-Jewish attitudes since antiquity usually identify first the emergence of anti-Judaism, and then its development into antisemitism somewhere between the Middle Ages and the nineteenth century. David Nirenberg, however, argued that anti-Judaism is a category of thinking, a way to interpret the world and shape criticism, running through history from ancient Egypt to modern times. Anti-Judaism is thus a tool in debate against the opponent, who is accused of being or behaving like a Jew; such accusations are divorced from real Jews, and their content changes with the context.[9] Similarly, Sara Lipton has argued that medieval art started to produce negative representations of Jews linked to debates within Christianity: the aim was not to vilify Jews, nor were the images a reflection of anti-Jewish hatred. Rather, they played a role in the process of Christians wrestling with "the relationship between physical perception and spiritual truth."[10] Both schemata of thought and representation, however, came to have a negative impact on real Jews by fostering and entrenching anti-Jewish attitudes among Christians.

Regardless of our preferred dating of the beginnings of antisemitism, and despite the undoubted features distinguishing Nazi and neo-Nazi antisemitism from earlier anti-Jewish attitudes, there is certainly an underlying continuity between modernity and what came before. Modern antisemitism draws on entrenched stereotypes that were created in the Middle Ages and have persisted, even though it can reshape them and invest them with new meaning.[11] The key antisemitic stereotypes still in existence today that originated in the Middle Ages include the ritual murder charge, the negative association of Jews with money, conspiracy theories, and alleged Jewish physical traits.

The medieval Catholic Church built Christianity on a strong anti-Jewish base. Early Christian leaders developed strategies to distinguish the newly forming Christian communities from Jews, since that distinction was not understood by many adherents of the emerging new faith. Separating the two communities did not merely entail delineating distinct practices, such as Christian fasting as opposed to Jewish fasting, but also hard-wired a violent rejection of Judaism into Christianity: a violent imposition of boundaries, denigration of Jews, and a Christian fashioning of Jewish practices as sinful.[12] Jewish scripture was appropriated as the basis of Christianity, and Christians claimed to have replaced Jews as the true Israel. Jews were blamed for rejecting and killing Christ. Supersession therefore was a basic tenet of Christian theology, which set up a long-term dynamic of Christian anti-Judaism. It cemented the idea of the inferiority of Jews, who were to be subordinate to Christians, which was reinforced and developed in multiple ways. Canon law, for example, progressively prohibited many forms of interaction between Jews and Christians, such as eating, drinking, and bathing together, and having Christian wet nurses in Jewish homes; it prescribed distinguishing clothing for Jews, and, while encouraging conversion to Christianity, made conversion to Judaism punishable by death.[13] The continued existence of Judaism posed a problem for medieval thinkers. While Augustine's solution of Jews being witnesses to the truth of Christianity held good for a while, at the height of Christian triumphalism the notion that all remaining Jews would convert at the end of times seemed unsatisfactory. Thus, explanations for Jewish unwillingness to convert insisted on the Jews' stubborn, blind, obstinate nature, or their lack of reason that made them subhuman. Medieval sermons were replete with the notion of Jews as killers of Christ and conditioned the population to regard Jews in a negative light.[14] Representations of Jews as the enemy of Christians came to feature regularly in diverse texts; by the thirteenth century, it was also increasingly present in imagery, from cathedral sculpture to illuminated manuscripts. Linked to new socio-economic and theological developments—such as a monetized mercantile economy that necessitated moneylending, the focus on Christ's humanity in devotion, and the doctrine of the real presence in the Eucharist—Jews started to be portrayed as a danger in the contemporary world. The charges of desecrating the host,

Alleged host desecration, as depicted on the winged altarpiece at the Church of the Holy Blood in Pulkau, tempera on wood, Master of Pulkau, Lower Austria, c. 1510–1525

Depiction of the alleged ritual murder of Simon of Trento, woodcut from the *Nuremberg Chronicle*, 1493

of ritual murder, and of usury presented Jews as actively trying to harm Christians.

From the mid-twelfth century, the ritual murder charge was leveled against Jews: that they killed Christian children in a manner imitating the crucifixion. In its first iteration by Thomas of Monmouth in the purported case of William of Norwich, this ritual killing is motivated by a Jewish prophecy to regain the land of Israel by sacrificing a Christian child each year. Similar accusations multiplied, but their details were fluid, and soon ritual murder was coupled to the blood libel: the allegation that Jews need Christian blood to relieve Jewish male menstruation, or to prepare the Passover matzah, or for various other purported uses.[15] Frederick II and Pope Innocent IV both issued refutations of such a charge, but—similarly to later reasoned opposition—this did not dispel the myth. Local cults grew up around many alleged victims, such as Hugh of Lincoln and Simon of Trent. Local bishops and clerics promoted these cults, although the papacy did not canonize the supposed martyrs. By the late sixteenth century, the papacy approved the cult of Simon.[16] Ritual murder trials still took place in Europe as recently as the late nineteenth century in Hungary and the early twentieth century in Kiev. Accusations of ritual murder resurfaced, for example, in Russia, Hungary, and some Islamic countries in the twenty-first century.

Medieval Christians created the connection between Jews and money, blaming Jews for usury.[17] Many medieval polities prohibited Jewish participation in numerous professions, limiting the sphere of economic activities for Jews, while trade and moneylending were open to them and increasingly necessary in the developing monetary economy. The Catholic Church tried to eliminate Christian lending at interest (initially branding all collection of interest as usury) in a context where there was a great need for capital. Ecclesiastical disapproval of and popular hostility to moneylenders then produced the image of the greedy, grasping, ruthless Jew, reinforced by visual imagery of Jews with moneybags. Jews were also targeted as symbols of royal authority. Since Jews were often in the service of kings and under their protection, medieval accusations also included the charge that Jews influenced and manipulated rulers, which can be seen as the precursor of more modern allegations that Jews dominate society or rule the world secretly. Conspiracy theories grew in the late medieval period: in 1321, Jews were accused of planning to poison Christians in concert with lepers, and then, in the plague years from 1348, they were blamed for causing the plague by poisoning wells, despite papal and imperial interventions against such claims. In the later Middle Ages, Jews were also accused of conspiring with Muslim military foes of Christians. They were thus depicted as deceitful and of questionable loyalty.[18]

Medieval representations are also the ultimate source of the hooked-nose racial stereotype, although in the Middle Ages the meaning of the visual sign was different.[19] Large beaked noses have served as a visual marker of bestiality, irrationality, and evil for a long time. They were used to designate devils and a variety of villains before they started to be applied to Jews in the 1160s and 1170s. This transfer did not at first signal ethnic stereotyping, but rather moral condemnation. At first, Jewish tormentors and killers of Christ were represented in this way, while Hebrew prophets, for example, were not. By the mid-thirteenth century, this visual marker was also applied to various contemporary Jews. In modern times, the hooked nose came to be understood as both an ethnic characteristic and a sign of evil, often in relation to money.

Thus, the composite antisemitic trope of the Jew as responsible for the ills of society, a danger to the social body, and intent on harming non-Jewish members of society ultimately derives from medieval roots.

Screenshot of an antisemitic Facebook post by the former head of the Freedom Party of Austria (FPÖ) and future vice-chancellor (2017-19) Heinz-Christian Strache, August 18, 2012

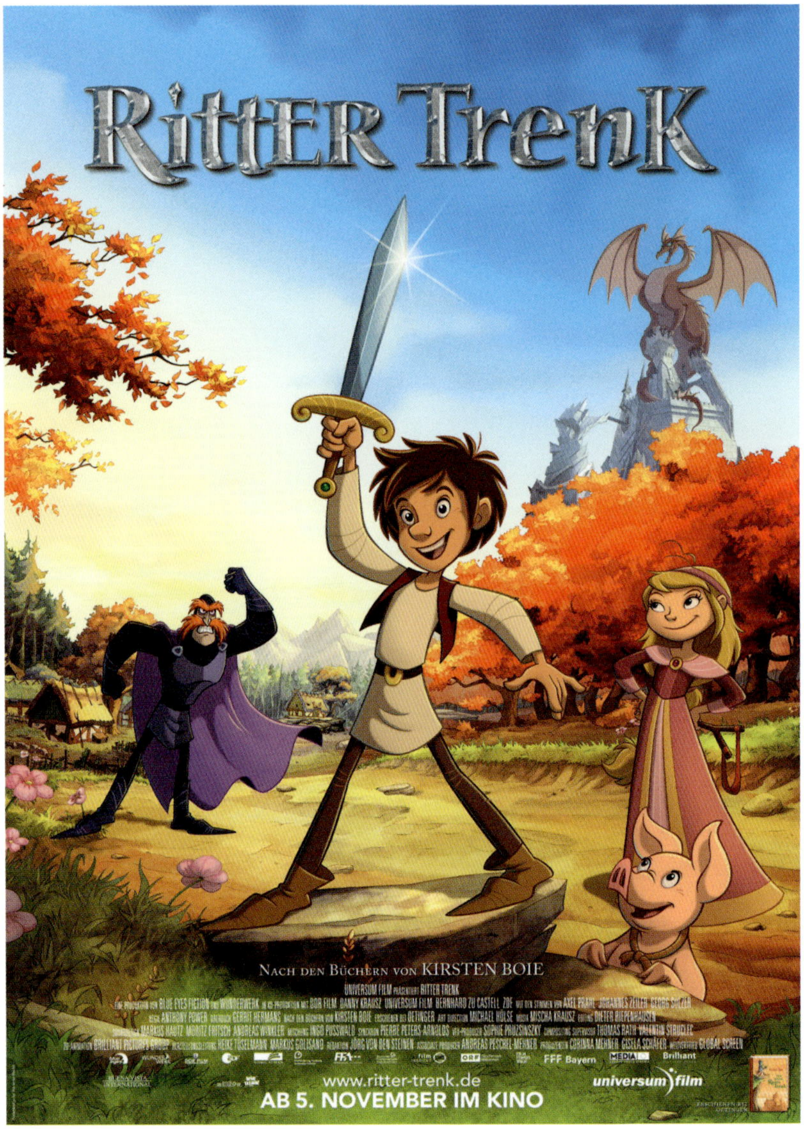

Poster for the animated film *Ritter Trenk* based on the book series *Der kleine Ritter Trenk* by Kristen Boie, 2016

From *Der kleine Ritter Trenk* to *Game of Thrones*

The Middle Ages for all age groups

Siegrid Schmidt

"What does the term 'Middle Ages' conjure up for you?" Most schoolchildren and students reply with "knights and castles," followed by plagues and popes, crusades, kings, dragons, witches, and burning at the stake. All of this is associated with the time between the classical and the modern ages. The term Middle Ages for this particular period in (central) European history goes back to the humanism of the sixteenth century, which sought a chronological structure for history, dividing it into Antiquity, Middle Ages, and the Modern Era. The images that these "middle ages" invoke today, however, have their origins mainly in the eighteenth and nineteenth centuries. At that time, two extreme views evolved: during the Enlightenment and neoclassical period, the Middle Ages were seen as a dark and backward period; for the Romantics, by contrast, it was at the root of their own cultural (and later also national) development and hence a bright, longed-for time that shaped their identity.

This essay looks at the way these concepts and constructs are still encountered today, but also how they have changed. It concludes with some thoughts as to why the Middle Ages as a whole, beyond the knights and castles, retain their fascination.

The Middle Ages for infants

Even in their earliest years, children are already confronted with the Middle Ages. Knights and castles are a popular motif in board picture books, with pages full of colorfully dressed people crowding around the castle and in the castle courtyard, or feasting in the banquet hall. There are merchants, tournaments, dragons, hunting, and banquets—all without any need for words. It sounds chaotic, but the attention of the young viewers is drawn to specific figures: "Can you find Kunibert the monk, the happy court jester, the damsel Katharina, the squire Jacob, and the naughty castle cat?"[1], friendly figures for children to identify with, representatives of different groups, without any judgment or negative attributes. The Middle Ages in this picture book offer some heroic challenges, but everything remains light and pleasant.

The Middle Ages for schoolchildren

The nursery is the next place for researching the Middle Ages, for this is where we find everything, from dragons that (unlike their past representations) have become friendly, helpful creatures—and not just in the form of cuddly toys—to armor and other medieval accoutrements. The bookcase contains books and magazines about jousting tournaments, crusaders, castles, feasts, and everyday life in the Middle Ages. On their own, or with their parents' help, children can build a Lego or Playmobil castle, and on rainy days or at bedtime they are read stories about knights and dragons. But these bold knights—be they called Arthur, Siegfried, or "der kleine Ritter Trenk"[2]—are barely ten years old and fight their battles with wooden swords. The more bloody battles will come later, when they are older.

At school, the fledgling medievalists may sometimes encounter other, more earnest knights—in sagas or historical novels from the last century for young readers, such as *Die Nibelungen* by Auguste Lechner,[3] for example. Traditional gender roles are explicitly perpetuated in these renditions, for instance when the heroines of the *Nibelungenlied*, Brunhild and Kriemhild, are introduced and their traits and challenges explained.[4] More recent chivalric tales now often feature equally talented and entitled young heroines,[5] but they still fail to be "promoted" to being featured in the title of the stories.

Even more fun than old stories are board games involving the quests of King Arthur and his Knights of the Round Table, or computer games on various platforms. Medieval props abound in these fantasy worlds: armor, (laser) swords, and all kinds of fortresses, castles, and princesses to be freed from the claws of (not so friendly) dragons.

Young adults and the medieval fascination

Teenagers today are primarily focused on electronic media. The way these media portray the Middle Ages—in terms of mood, characters, props, and architecture—shapes the adolescent view of those times. It starts with the sheer endless array of computer games, which either borrow constructed empires from books, films, or television series, such as *Game of Thrones*, *Star Wars*, and *Lord of the Rings*, or, alternatively, develop entirely new fantasy worlds or galaxies. In online games, players are invited to "create villages, forge bonds, conquer worlds" or to "raise an empire." Here, the warlike image of the Middle Ages predominates. The role of women in many of these computer games is also often highly problematic. They are either "decorative" princesses, or grubby, hardworking peasants. In one marketing video,

Release day of *Cataclysm*, an expansion of the multiplayer online video game *World of Warcraft*, Berlin, 2010

Still from *Monty Python and the Holy Grail*, directed by Terry Gilliam and Terry Jones, UK, 1975

the medieval lady appears as a knightly dominatrix. These roles suggest that women are subject to a high degree of control from outside forces in a world dominated by men.

Young-adult fiction with tie-ins to medieval themes still has an important role. For younger readers, the Harry Potter books (also appearing in other media) are a major influence, while for older children such novels often form the literary basis for the aforementioned computer games. More of a niche product are literary works like Martin Grzimek's *Tristan: Roman um Treue, Liebe und Verrat*,[6] which retells the old Tristan and Iseult legend specially for this age group.

Although no longer new, one medium that still influences perceptions of the Middle Ages, not only among adolescents but also for their parents and grandparents, is the cinema. Films have featured historical and literary themes, medieval figures, and events from the Middle Ages for a good hundred years. For example, several films in the 1950s told the story of King Arthur and his Knights of the Round Table; then, in 1975, we had the inimitable *Monty Python and the Holy Grail*, and a

3D version, *King Arthur: Legend of the Sword*, in 2017. An example of the amalgamation of historical facts and fiction is the film version of Noah Gordon's *The Physician*.[7] Set in the eleventh century, it describes the adventures of the young Englishman Robert, who travels to the city of Isfahan to study the noble art of medicine with the—historically authentic—polymath Avicenna. Since he would not be accepted there as a Christian, he circumcises himself and, as a Jew, is at least tolerated and able to study.

Clear traces of medieval themes are often found in another medium, also dating back about a century, which—although having changed

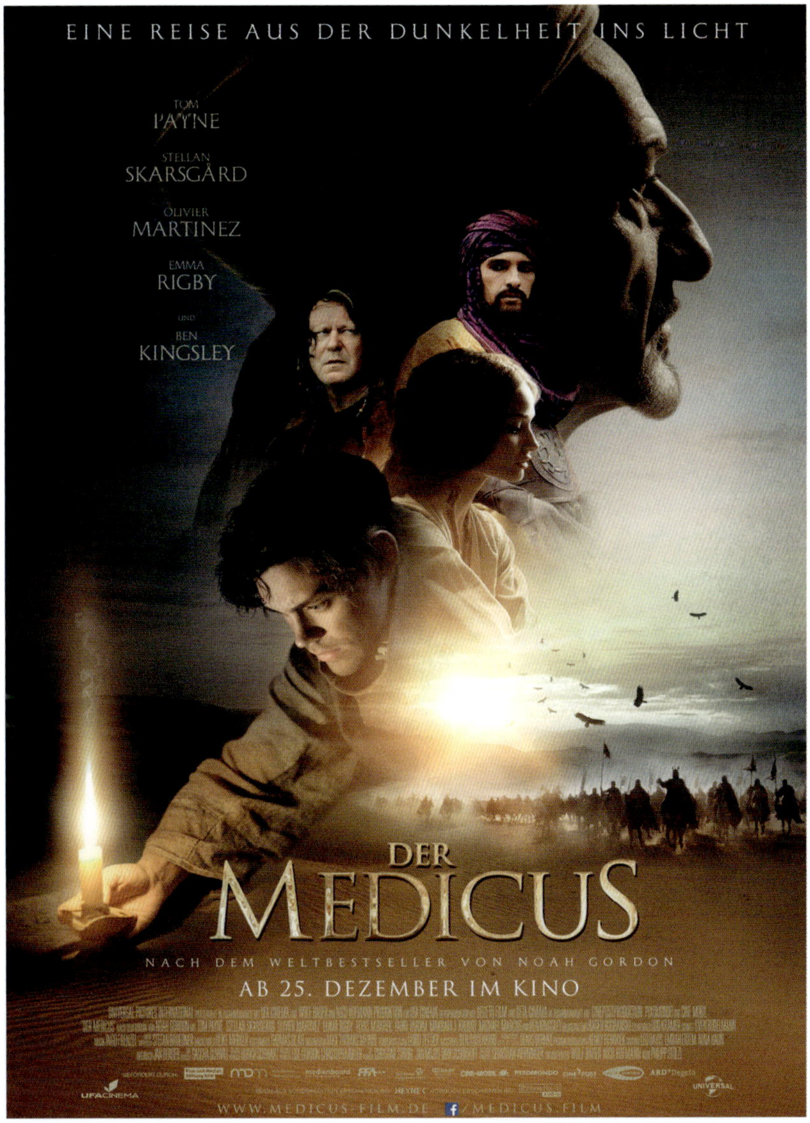

Poster for the feature film *The Physician*, directed by Philipp Stölzl, Germany, 2013

considerably over time—is very popular with young adults: the graphic novel. In Germany, the tradition started with the *Sigurd* comic book series (1953), continuing with Disney's *The Sword in the Stone* (1963), and is now represented by a flood of fantasy works, often taking cues from the Nibelungen saga or the tradition of Nordic gods in general.

In higher education, there are lots of courses with tie-ins to the Middle Ages: history, literature, art and theater history, theology, philosophy, history of law, etc. The concept of the medieval period developed until then now undergoes a change, or is at least fleshed out through academic study, not least in the realization that our knowledge is hazier than we might have thought. Literature, (book) art, and chronicles can have a cultural fascination but still remain somehow alien.

Participants in the Landshut Wedding dressed as mercenaries, Bavaria/Germany, 2005

The Middle Ages for grown-ups

In practically all areas of culture, in institutions, and in public life, our pre-formed ideas about the Middle Ages live on in a variety of guises. In the public sphere, there are the countless medieval pageants and fairs, tournaments, reenactments of battles or other historical events, and live action role-playing. Popular examples in Germany include the Kaltenberg Knights Tournament, the medieval festival at Burghausen Castle, and the Landshut Wedding, based on a historical event (the marriage of George of Bavaria to Hedwig Jagiellon in 1475) which is recreated at intervals with around 2,000 participants. In all of these activities, the human play instinct is always the focus. Play is a sociocultural act that is carried out for its own sake and essentially manifests itself in one of four ways: as combat or competition, as a game of chance, as thrill-seeking, or as mimicry, i.e. role-playing and dressing up. The last-named is of central significance in our context, but all other types of play can also be found at medieval festivals.[8] These play variants always have the potential to reflect both the light, cultural Middle Ages—for example in role-play with music and dancing—and the dark, brutal Middle Ages, perhaps with games of chance and intoxication.

A completely different type of dress-up game relating to the Middle Ages can be found on the stages of Europe's theaters and opera houses. Passion and mystery plays, which have their roots in the Middle Ages and are still performed today in modern adaptations, form a link with the above-mentioned events in the public arena. Operas, comedies, and tragedies with medieval themes have been around since at least the seventeenth century. Examples include classics such as *Götz von Berlichingen*, *William Tell*, or *Faust*. The medieval Nibelungen saga, in particular, exerted a great fascination for nineteenth-century playwrights, with adaptations by Richard Wagner and Friedrich Hebbel—although the representation of the Middle Ages in theater and opera was based less on their literary sources and more on the poetic and ideological mainstream at the time of their creation. More recent plays with a reference to the Middle Ages in their title have often focused more on current sociopolitical themes, as, for example, *Merlin oder Das wüste Land* by Tankred Dorst and Ursula Ehler, or Christoph

Hein's *Ritter der Tafelrunde*.[9] The authors use medieval literary figures not to present historical images but rather as vehicles for addressing issues of our time.

Exhibitions and museums tend to have less explicit reference to the modern day. Medieval rulers and dynasties, for example, have been a popular subject of exhibitions since the mid-1970s: the Stauffers, Babenbergs, Kuenrings, Habsburgs, rulers of the Holy Roman Empire; and 2019 featured countless exhibitions about the Holy Roman Emperor Maximilian I to mark the 500th anniversary of his death. Precious original artifacts and informative installations highlight the art and culture of the Middle Ages, offering a constructive and less gloomy view of the era. Reinforcing (national) identity and self-assurance is at least part of the motivation for these shows, along with entertainment and commercial considerations.

Conclusion

This essay cites some typical ways in which the European Middle Ages continue to be relevant today. It provides an overview of the diverse media and material presentation of the era for the various different age groups, while also including occasional references to the conceptual and theoretical diversity. It seems that the Middle Ages can serve as a symbol for almost anything. They can represent a context for friendly superheroes, cruelty, backwardness, and brutality, or they can offer a fascinating environment with courtly culture and literature, chivalry, and gallantry. In this way, the contrasting images of the Middle Ages, both light and dark, are perpetuated, while their prevalence in all media and among all target groups is further expanded. A third view of the Middle Ages is added, that of friendly knights and helpful dragons—at least for younger readers and viewers. Signs of a fourth dimension, namely the deliberate and critical discussion of gender roles and the image of women, are still hard to find across all target groups. These discussions may sometimes be found in academic discourse about such texts and other cultural phenomena, but a critical awareness is non-existent within the works themselves or at best only marginally acknowledged.

In all these manifestations, the Middle Ages—or rather the many different ways in which this era is perceived—serve as a projection space for a number of needs of the modern and post-modern age. It offers friendly and successful identifying figures, and its literature contains characters and adventures that are exotic enough to distract us from everyday life, yet familiar enough to integrate them in our mental and cultural paradigms, be it at a concert with medieval music and song, or in an opera or play. Medieval role-playing provides an opportunity to put into practice all types of play and dressing up that the various age and target groups expect from an ideal play setting. Many want such role-playing to be as loud, raucous, warlike, and rough as possible. A smaller group just seeks a more authentic, down-to-earth way of life. All of this is available in analogue and real-time versions, but also virtually and at home. Does this make the Middle Ages the perfect past for the present and future?

Iron Throne and costumes in the touring exhibition based on HBO's internationally acclaimed television series *Game of Thrones*, 2019

Juda Guntzenhauser, son of Leiser, was a doctor in Vienna. In this document of May 24, 1403, he swears under oath to refrain from practicing medicine.

From "Kammergut" to "Hofbefreiung"

Jews in Vienna in the early modern era

Domagoj Akrap

The Vienna Gesera—the expulsion and murder of the Viennese Jews in 1420/21—put an end to the Jewish community in Vienna, which had existed for almost two hundred years. For the next century and a half, only individual Jews were allowed to settle in Vienna, and then only for a limited time. As early as 1438, Duke Albert V, who had previously ordered the terrible pogrom, allowed the Jew Isserlein to move freely in Austria, stating in justification that he was entirely innocent and uninvolved in any of the accusations made against the Jewish community at the time of the Vienna Gesera.[1] That same year, the Medical University of Vienna complained to the mayor about alleged charlatans, naming Jews and converts among others.[2]

A legal basis for the limited settlement of Jews was established by the Papal Bull of September 20, 1451, which allowed Jews to settle in the country for the mutual benefit of Jews and Christians. Emperor Frederick III (1452–1493) was generally considered "pro-Jewish," which meant merely that Jews under his protection were safeguarded against hostility and the threat of persecution—while the emperor raked in substantial revenue for tolerating them. Jews did occasionally settle in Vienna during the fifteenth century under protection of letters of safe conduct issued by the rulers. For example, in 1454, a Jewish doctor in

Vienna with a royal letter of safe conduct was objected to by the Medical University, which demanded that he be prevented from practicing.[3] Since the early fifteenth century, the Medical University had been hostile towards Jewish and even converted doctors, because it feared competition from them and above all wished to assert its supremacy as the only authorized education establishment. Jewish doctors were attacked and involved in court cases.[4]

Under Frederick's son Maximilian I, the Jews were expelled from Styria, Carinthia, and Carniola after a long tug-of-war between the emperor and the territorial estates. The emperor was compensated by the estates for the loss of revenue from Jewish taxes. In contrast to the expulsion from Vienna in 1421, this time the Jews were able to sell their possessions and call in outstanding debts. Most of the expelled Jews were settled in other imperial territories in the Austrian eastern borderlands—Marchegg, Eisenstadt, and Kőszeg (now in Hungary), where the emperor, who was permanently short of funds, was still able to benefit from Jewish taxes.[5]

From the early sixteenth century, Jews living near Vienna regularly came to the city on business. In 1511, the emperor promulgated a decree stating that special clothing had to be worn inside the city but was not required outside the city walls. At this time, there was still no established Jewish community in Vienna. However, the number of Jews grew steadily from the early sixteenth century, so much so that the estates regularly protested against their presence and demanded their expulsion. In a petition to the emperor in 1515, for example, they claimed that the Jews had settled in Vienna and other places as if they had the right to do so and asked the emperor to expel them. These and other complaints by the estates were repeated in subsequent years. They always stressed that the Jews and their "practices" brought ruin and suffering to the "common man" and that their commerce and usury in Vienna brought disadvantage to Christians.[6]

During the reign of Emperor Ferdinand I (archduke from 1521 to 1564), there was a gradual transition from the concept of Jews as the emperor's "Kammergut" (effectively his "vassals," i.e. part of his domain) to the modern notion of Jews—men and in rare instances also women—as "hofbefreit," that is, suppliers to the court with certain privileges bestowed on them by the emperor. In the order of May 18, 1536, the emperor still spoke of "cammerguet," referring to those Jews who were legally entitled to stay in Austria.[7] As such they were distinct from "foreign Jews," who were only allowed to reside for a short time, often just one day, and forbidden from conducting any kind of business. A privilege for the entire Jewish population, as was customary in the Middle Ages, did not exist for Vienna. The local ruler, who in Vienna in those times was usually also the emperor, issued privileges for individual Jews and their families, in most cases as a result of a personal interest. These privileges were the only way for Jews to settle legally in the country and to hope for the ruler's protection.

Jewish business activities were still centered on moneylending, a profession they had been assigned since the Middle Ages, but there was a gradual shift towards trade, which in the sixteenth and seventeenth centuries became the main focus. The principal commodities were animal products, such as wool, leather, meat, and also live animals. Those with higher privileges also traded in semi-luxury products, such as expensive fabrics, jewelry, and precious stones. Around the mid-sixteenth century, some Jews were already trading in scrap silver for the imperial mint.[8] For example, in recognition of his years of service at the mint, a certain Moses was awarded a court privilege on January 18, 1543, which enabled him to conduct business in Austria.

The "Judenordnungen" (regulations and decrees relating to Jews), which were partly issued to protect the Jews, but also to appease the estates in their calls to have the Jews expelled, were occasionally followed by the expulsion of "unfree" Jews, that is to say Jews without a court privilege.[9]

A decree by Ferdinand I in 1551 created a requirement for Jews in Austria to wear identifying symbols. The aim of this discriminatory regulation was to make Jews recognizable, after they had become increasingly assimilated with Christians in terms of clothing and appearance. Jews were now required to wear a "yellow circle" on their left breast whenever they were in an inhabited area. Only when traveling were they exempt from this requirement, to prevent them becoming a target for attacks. In practice, this regulation was not fully complied with and was more a reflection of the desire of some estates than the

Wir Ferdinand von Gottes genaden Römischer / zu Hungern vnd Behaim ꝛc. Künig / Infant in Hispanien / Ertzhertzog

Decree by Ferdinand I requiring Jews to wear identifying symbols, Vienna, 1551

real situation. Privileged Jewish families, for example, requested exemption from the regulation, while others took the risk of a fine and simply ignored it.

In the second half of the sixteenth century, a Jewish community gradually began to develop in Vienna. It consisted initially of a few families with court privileges. The emperor granted this status to economically powerful Jews, whose financial and fiscal contributions were of value to him. Above all, they helped to finance the drawn-out Turkish wars and the Thirty Years War. The privilege was enjoyed by the holder and normally his family and servants as well and placed them under the direct legal protection of the emperor. Through this close connection to the imperial court, an elite class gradually formed within the Jewish population. As the privileges could also be withdrawn at any time, however, their position remained precarious in spite of their relative wealth.

In 1571, Emperor Maximilian II allowed seven privileged Jewish families to live in Vienna. Less than ten years later, a Jewish cemetery was laid out in Rossau (Oberer Werd). We do not know precisely when the site was acquired. The oldest gravestone that can be clearly dated is from 1582. The cemetery in the northern outskirts, now Seegasse in the 9th district, is the only remaining material culture evidence of Vienna's second Jewish community.[10] In that same year, a Jewish delegation described itself in a petition to the Lower Austrian government as "the entire permitted Jewish community here," which suggests that the community was well established and institutionalized.[11] From a source in 1596, we know that by this time there were two synagogues (shuls) in Vienna. They were not synagogues as we understand them today, but prayer rooms in the residences of privileged Jews. Each privilege stated

Triumphal arch created by the Jews of Vienna in honor of Archduke Matthias, 1608, engraving by Georg Keller

Following double page: Old Jewish cemetery at Seegasse 9-11 in the 9th district of Vienna, 2020

whether the holder was allowed to have a synagogue or not. In 1611, Veit Munk attempted to purchase a house to establish a synagogue but was refused permission from the highest level. Eleven years later, the Viennese Jews once again attempted to acquire a building for a synagogue. In October 1622, Emperor Ferdinand II issued an edict acceding to the request. However, only a year later the municipal authorities appealed against the edict, because the Jews had exceeded the authorized limit and had "even had the effrontery almost to erect a temple."[12]

On the occasion of Archduke Matthias's visit to pay homage as the new governor of the Austrian territories in the summer of 1608, the Jewish community publicly honored him with its own triumphal arch. An eyewitness reported the event in a rhyming verse, which describes how the Jewish community celebrated the archduke in ceremonial clothing under a canopy with the Talmud and Torah near Vienna's Rotenturmstrasse.[13]

By the start of the seventeenth century, the Viennese Jews were living in the center of the city, renting houses from Christians. They lived mostly around Kienmarkt (now Desider-Friedmann-Platz), a part of the city some distance from the main thoroughfares leading to the city gates, but nevertheless close enough to Hoher Markt and the Rotenturm, the starting point of roads northward to Bohemia and Moravia. Most of them were privileged or worked for privileged Jews. The wealthy families of the privileged Jews had leading positions in the community and were its external representatives. These families were often interrelated by marriage, leading to the formation of family networks extending far beyond the immediate region. This formation of elites was typical of the early modern era and can also be found in Prague, which had the largest Jewish community in central Europe at the time.

Family networks–the Munks and the Lucernas

The Munk family from Prague is thought to have arrived in Vienna in the 1570s and was among the first families to be granted a privilege by the emperor. Members of this family, already highly influential in Bohemia, very soon assumed leading positions in the emerging Viennese community. Samuel Phöbus ben Moses Lämmel Theomim (in documents Veit Munk), who with his brother Salomon was the first to move

Court privilege for Gertraut Munk, the only known privilege awarded to a Jewish woman, 1620

Wir Ferdinand, von Gottes gnaden erwelter Römischer Kaiser, zu allen zeiten mehrer des Reichs, in Germanien, zu Hungern, Behaimb, Dalmatien, Croatien und Sclavonien etc. König, Erzherzog zu Osterreich, herzog zu Burgundi, zu Braband, zu Steyr, zu Kärnten, zu Crain, zu Lützemburg, zu Wirtemberg, Ober und Nider Schlesien, Fürst zu Schwaben, Marggrave des heiligen Römischen Reichs zu Burgau, zu Märhern, Ober und Nider Lausniz, gefürster Grave zu Habspurg, zu Tyrol, zu Pfierdt, zu Kyburg und zu Görz, Landgrave in Elsass, Herr auf der Windischen Marckh, zu Porttenau und zu Salins etc. Bekhennen mit disem brief offentlich [illegible]

[illegible]

inserirten [illegible]

Gravestones of the Lucerna family in the old Jewish cemetery at Seegasse 9–11 in the 9th district of Vienna, 2020

to Vienna, became spokesperson of the entire community of privileged Jews on January 5, 1603.[14] In the document from Emperor Matthias confirming his privilege, he was given permission to establish a synagogue. The fact that he already possessed several previous privileges and had permission to run a private synagogue is evident from documents issued in 1595 and 1609, and from a mention in 1596 of a "Veit Müncka judenschuel zu Wien."[15] His son Nathan Theomim (also Veit Munk the Younger) studied in Kraków and in 1612 became a rabbi in Eisenstadt before going to Worms and then returning to Vienna as a rabbi in 1622.

Veit Munk's wife Gertraut Munk (née Wendl) was an exceptional personality. Quite early on, she was operating independently of her husband and concluded business transactions in her own name. The first mention of her name is on a Yiddish receipt from 1591, issued by her brother-in-law Salomon Munk. It is interesting to note that the receipt is not signed by Gertraut herself, although she was authorized to do so, but by Salomon on her behalf, perhaps acting as a proxy in her absence.[16] A large number of *laissez-passer* notes exist for the years after 1600, testifying to her lively business activities, with trips to Prague, Regensburg, the Palatinate, and Poland. Apart from moneylending, she traded in precious metals and probably had a jewelry business as well. She was also the holder of the only surviving court privilege for a Jewish woman.[17] It was issued in 1620 and included the right to live in Vienna and imperial territories, to conduct business, and to be exempt from paying special Jewish levies at annual fairs. The right to run a private synagogue was confirmed and extended to all places where she and other free Jews settled.

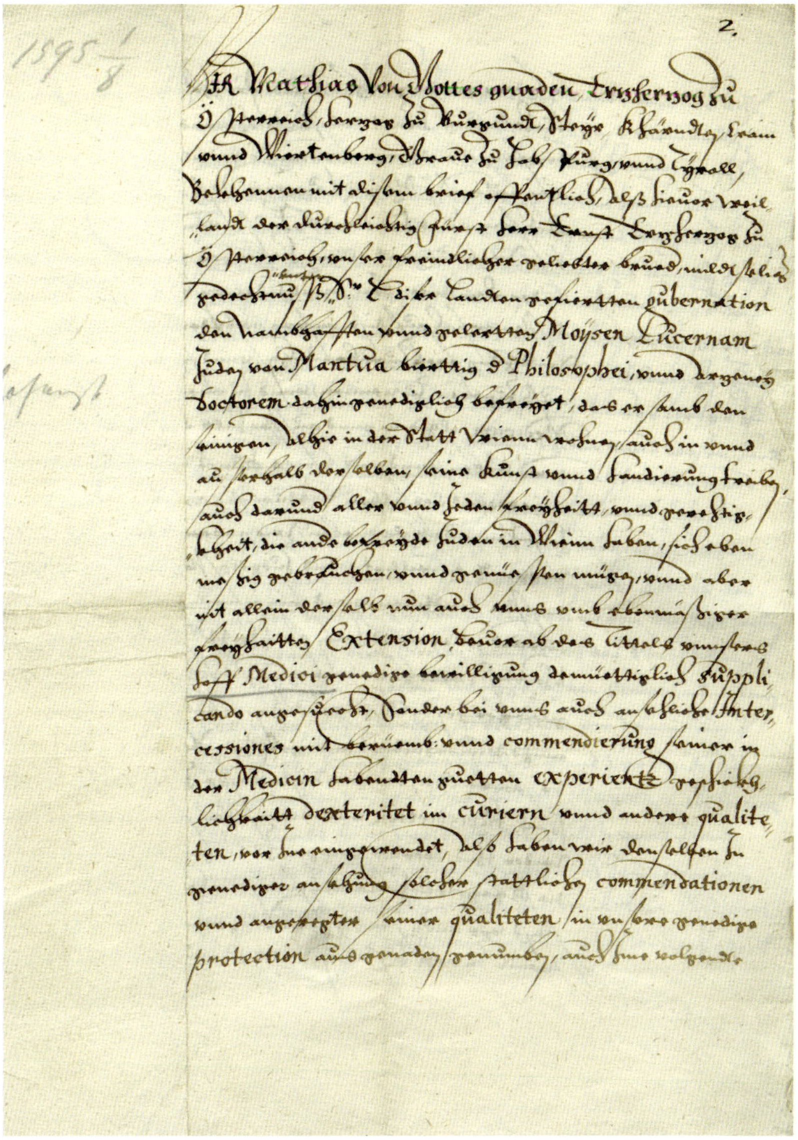

Moses Lucerna's appointment as court physician, August 1, 1595

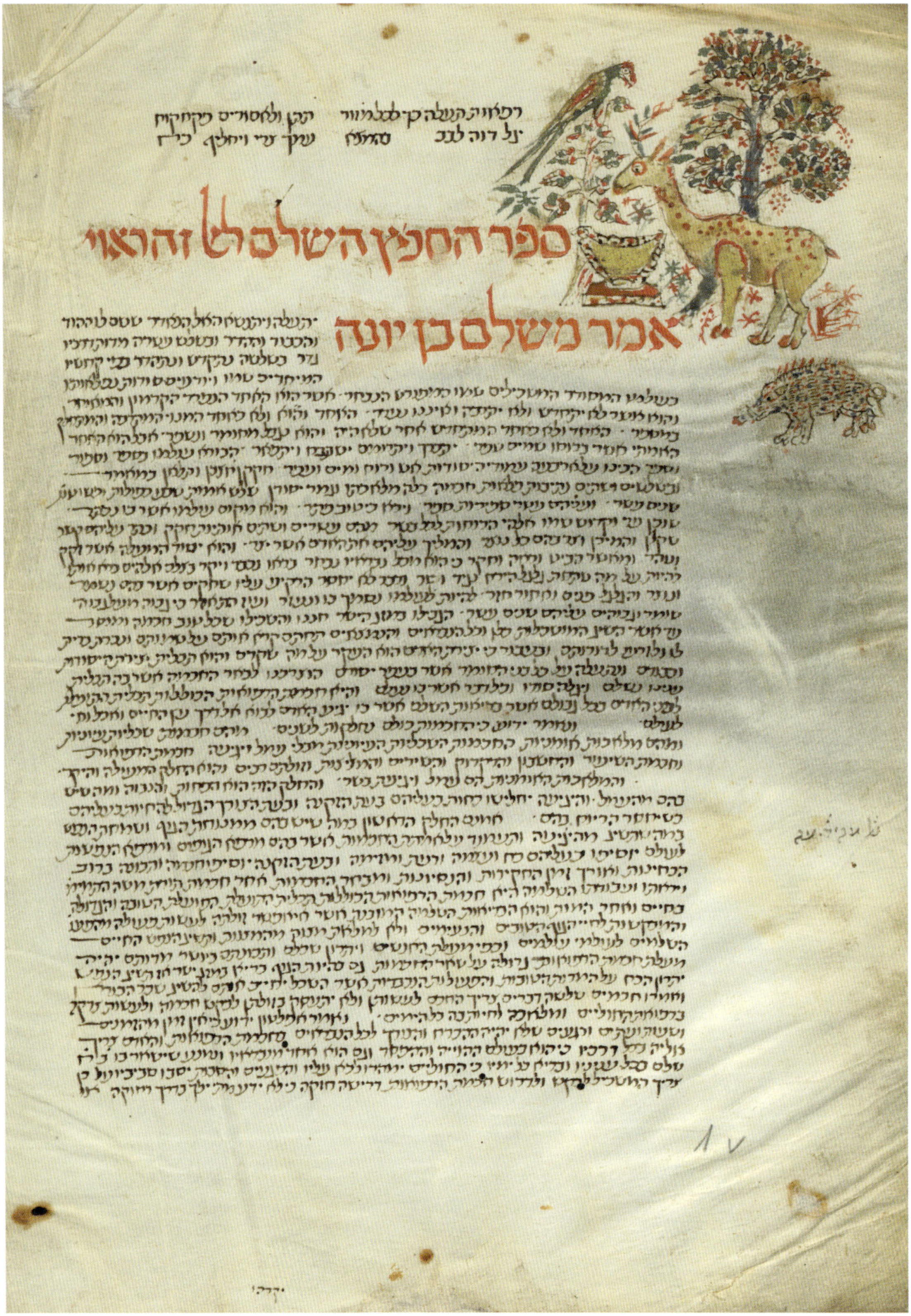

Rabbis were forbidden from excommunicating her. This last point is interesting, as it represents an interference in internal Jewish affairs, a common occurrence from the early modern period onward, when secular authorities increasingly used their superior financial power to assert themselves over the religious leaders in the Jewish community.

Moses Lucerna (Maor-Katan) arrived in Vienna at around the same time as the Munks. The family came from Italy, probably Mantua. Moses had studied medicine in Padua at one of the few universities to accept Jews at the time and initially practiced in Frankfurt. He left in 1576 and came to Vienna. In 1595, he was appointed court physician by Archduke Matthias. He married Kela, the sister-in-law of Gertraut Munk. Two of his sons also became doctors. The older one, Leo Lucerna (Yehuda Löb), held a triple doctorate and a special court privilege and for some time was also head of the community. Five Hebrew manuscripts in the Austrian National Library are from his personal collection, all but one with medical content. Leo Lucerna also cultivated the friendship of Sebastian Tengnagel, future prefect of the imperial court library, for whom he wrote a letter of recommendation in 1609 to the celebrated Jewish scholar Samuel Archivolti in Padua.[18] His brother Aron Lucerna was active in Prague as a high-ranking community physician just after the outbreak of the Thirty Years War. We also know from source material that he traded in coins.[19] His wife, too, was a member of the Munk family—she was the daughter of Gertraut, thereby further strengthening the ties between the two families. His impressive gravestone is decorated with a lion rampant, the symbol of doctors, and a small half-moon, possibly a reference to the family name, which means "small light."[20]

These two privileged families serve as examples of economic and social ascent at a time of transition, when a Jewish community began to re-establish itself in Vienna, even though its situation always remained precarious. They achieved their position not least thanks to their skillful marriage policy, the exploitation of family networks, and increasing mobility. Even after the Jewish district was established in Unterer Werd in 1625 by order of Emperor Ferdinand, these families remained among the elite of the Jewish community.

Medical manuscript owned by the Jewish doctor Leo Lucerna, 1415

A Sack Full of Letters: Insights into Everyday Jewish Life in 1619

The year is 1619, and war has been raging in central Europe for over a year. Since the crowning of Frederick V of the Palatinate as King of Bohemia, the cities of Prague and Vienna have been on opposite sides. The imperial residential city has been under siege for several weeks, and on top of all that an epidemic is spreading. On Friday, November 22, a mail carrier with letters from members of the Jewish community in Prague set off for Vienna. The bundle of forty-seven letters was probably intercepted en route and has only survived thanks to the fortunate circumstance that all of the letters were written in Hebrew or Judeo-German and as a result were not immediately destroyed. For centuries they remained untouched in the cellars of the imperial archive, until they were discovered and published in 1911 by Alfred Landau and Bernhard Wachstein. The letters provide a unique testimony to Jewish family history–a snapshot of everyday life in the communities of Prague and Vienna, including that of prominent families such as the Heller-Wallersteins, Hammerschlags, Auerbachs, and Maor-Katans (Lucernas). The contents are mostly personal and only occasionally make reference to the precarious political situation and the ongoing war and threat of disease. The main topics revolve around the wellbeing of family members, business in those uncertain times, matchmaking, or simply the desire to meet again–topics that are still typically found to this day in the private correspondence of people separated by circumstances, albeit now more likely to be in electronic form than in written letters.

Domagoj Akrap

Following double page: Judenplatz in 2020, with the Memorial to the Austrian Jewish Victims of the Shoah, the Lessing monument, and in the background the Jordanhaus with the anti-Jewish relief on its façade

Letter from Mirjam Lucerna, daughter of the court physician Moses Lucerna, to her sister-in-law in Vienna, 1619

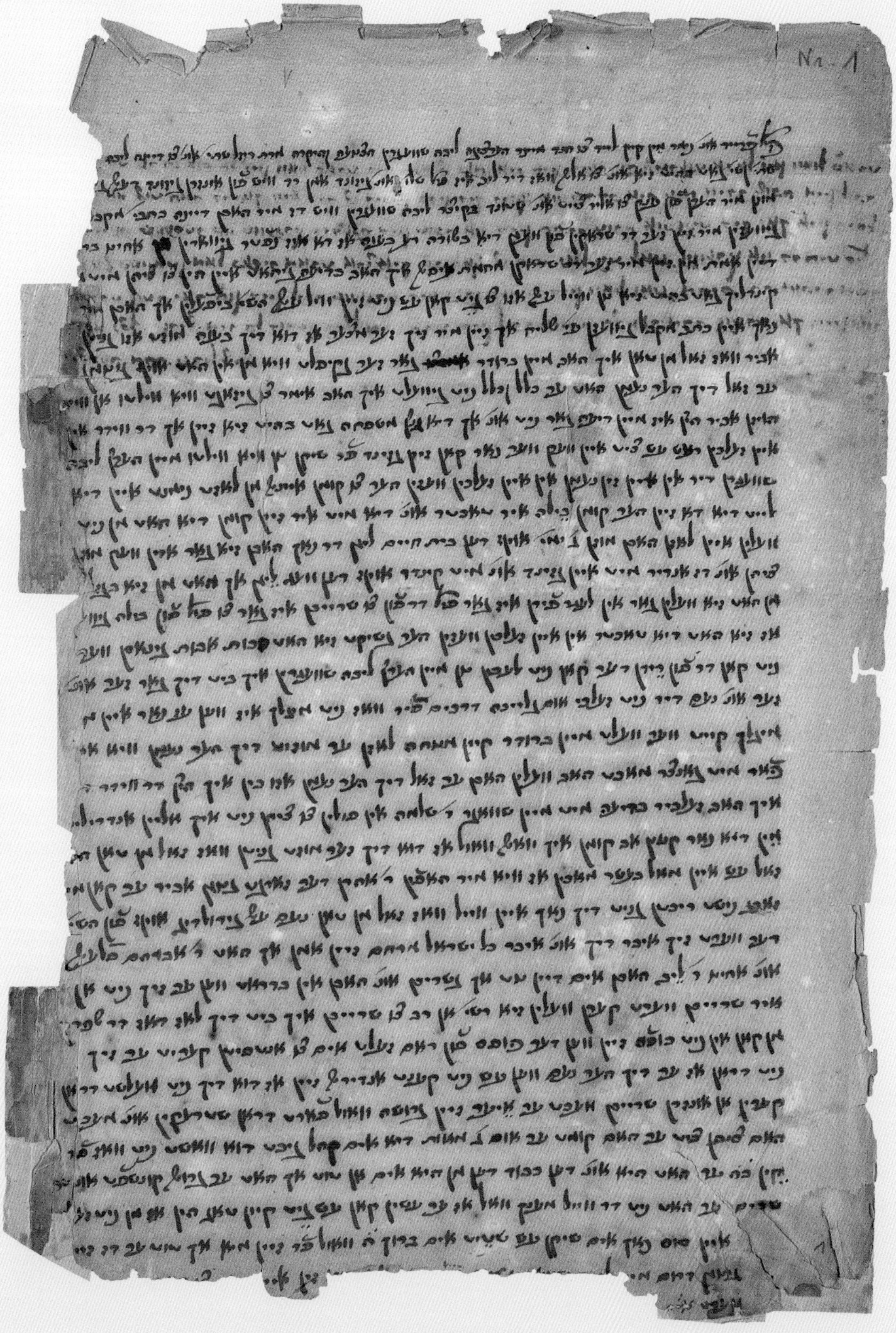

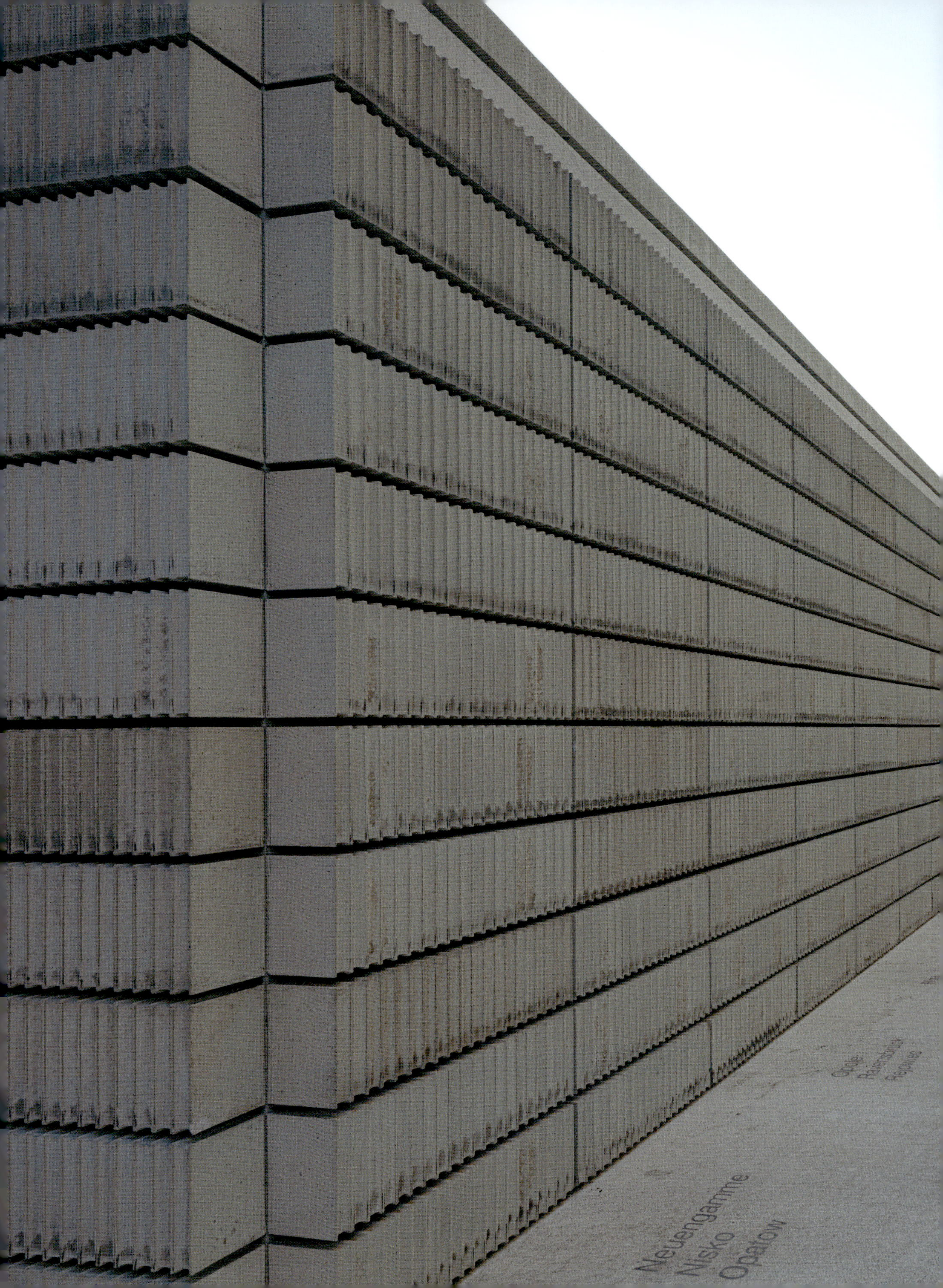
Neuengamme
Nisko
Opatow
Opole
Ravensbrück
Rejowiec

The Lessing Monument on Judenplatz: A Story from the Turbulent Twentieth Century

A statue of the German poet Gotthold Ephraim Lessing (1729-1781), a major representative of the Enlightenment and an ambassador for tolerance, stands today on the site of the Jewish quarter destroyed in 1421. The story of this statue in itself can be seen as symbolic for the turbulent history of the twentieth century. In the early years of that century, the Concordia Press Club–the oldest press club in the world, devoted continuously to democracy and freedom of the press–called for the erection of a monument to Lessing. A competition was held, resulting in the Viennese sculptor Siegfried Charoux being commissioned to create it. After a delay lasting several decades, the bronze statue created by him was installed on Judenplatz on June 15, 1935. In his inaugural speech, the deputy mayor Fritz Lahr–also deputy head of the largely antisemitic Vienna Heimwehr and a future National Socialist–announced that Judenplatz was to be renamed Lessingplatz. However, this plan was never implemented.[1] The Nazis melted down the statue in 1939. Charoux, who had emigrated to Great Britain in 1935 for political reasons, was invited by the Vienna city council in 1947 to recreate the Lessing monument. Again there were lengthy delays, and by the time the statue was finally unveiled on Morzinplatz in 1968, Charoux was no longer alive to witness it. On October 30, 1981, the statue was moved to its original site on Judenplatz, where it still stands today.

Astrid Peterle

The Lessing monument by Siegfried Charoux on Judenplatz, 2020

LESSING
SHOP
12

View of Judenplatz c. 1730 by Salomon Kleiner, colored reprint of an engraving, Vienna, 1856; visible near the right-hand edge of the picture is the façade of Judenplatz 8, which now houses Museum Judenplatz.

Judenplatz

Biography of an urban space

Astrid Peterle

After the Vienna Gesera, the expulsion and murder of the Jews of Vienna in 1420/21, all traces of Jewish life on Judenplatz remained, quite literally, buried for several centuries. Although the name Judenplatz became established in the sixteenth century and has remained until today, there was little awareness of the once vibrant life of the Jewish community in the Middle Ages until well into the twentieth century. It was not until the widespread public and political debate on the erection of a memorial to the Austrian Jewish victims of the Shoah and the archaeological excavations in the 1990s that the history of Vienna's first Jewish community was made visible again.

A place of buried history

It is thanks to archaeologists that knowledge about Judenplatz, which researchers had hitherto acquired solely from city maps and land registers, was considerably expanded and fleshed out. During the Roman era (first to fifth centuries), there was a legionary camp on the site of the present-day Judenplatz. The site was abandoned thereafter for several centuries. Jews began to settle in this central area of the city around the mid-thirteenth century at the latest. After their expulsion and murder in 1420/21, the synagogue in the center of the Jewish

Jordanhaus, Judenplatz 2,
with its anti-Jewish relief, 2020

quarter was razed to the ground with only the foundations remaining. Much of the masonry was used to construct new buildings for the University of Vienna, which as an institution had been most vocal in stirring up anti-Jewish feeling in the preceding years. The destruction of the synagogue left a pit, which was filled in with building rubble and waste.[1] The demolition of buildings at the eastern end of the present-day square created an open space, initially simply called the "new square in Judengasse."[2] A little later it became known as the "Schulhof"—with reference to the synagogue courtyard—but the name Judenplatz also came to be used increasingly, as documented in Michael Beheim's *Buch von den Wienern* from 1463.[3] This name can also be found on two city maps by Augustin Hirschvogel and Bonifaz Wolmuet in 1547. For a long time, Judenplatz was considered a typical example of a medieval city square. However, it only became an open square as a result of the structural changes following the Vienna Gesera and during the early modern period from the late fifteenth century. On an etching by Salomon Kleiner from the 1730s, the façade of house number 8, now the home of Museum Judenplatz, can be clearly seen, along with the recess in the street frontage indicating the site of the medieval synagogue courtyard.[4]

Apart from the name, the Jewish history of Judenplatz remained forgotten for many centuries. Only one building, the present-day Judenplatz 2, "Zum grossen Jordan," the oldest surviving building on the square, bore a reference to the Jewish community, or, more precisely, to its extinction. A previous building on this site belonged to the Jew Hocz until 1421. Georg Jordan built the new house in its place, possibly in 1497. The surviving original façade bears a relief, probably from the same time, which, in a reference to the owner's name, shows the baptism of Christ in the river Jordan. Below the relief is an anti-Jewish inscription in Latin alluding to the Vienna Gesera and speaking of a "flame of hate," which in 1421 avenged the "terrible crimes of the repulsive Hebrew dogs." Through the link with the baptismal scene, the burning of the Jews is thus interpreted as a cleansing and atonement. Following the fierce discussion about this anti-Jewish inscription in connection with the planned Shoah memorial in the 1990s, the Archdiocese of Vienna had a plaque placed on the wall of Judenplatz 6 in October 1998. Through this commemoration, it acknowledged the responsibility of Christians in the anti-Jewish pogroms and killings in the Middle Ages and drew parallels with the persecution of the Jews during the Nazi era. It does not, however, include any direct admission of guilt by the Church. The plaque merely mentions that "Christian preachers" in the Middle Ages spread "anti-Jewish superstitions" and thereby stirred up hatred against "Jews and their faith."

While the history of the Jews was forgotten and suppressed after the Vienna Gesera, Judenplatz developed into a place for business and entertainment. For centuries it was used as a market square, initially mainly for wood and green fodder, and then, in the nineteenth century, for fairs and the annual All Saints' market with booths and stalls.[5] As early as the seventeenth century, records confirm its regular use for fairground attractions and performances by street artists, such as tight-rope walkers.[6]

The pioneers of research on Vienna's first Jewish community

In the late nineteenth century, Jewish academics began to show an increased interest in researching and communicating Jewish history and culture, one result of which was the founding of the world's first Jewish museum in 1895. In the early twentieth century, three authors published important works on Vienna's first Jewish community in the Middle Ages. Their findings remained influential until well into the 1990s and were only updated due to the Judenplatz excavations and associated research by Jewish studies scholars, historians, and archaeologists. One of the main reasons that the study of written sources relating to medieval Jewish life in Vienna and Austria had been stalled for decades after the initial work of these three pioneers was no doubt the hiatus caused by the Shoah and the expulsion, persecution, and murder of Jewish academics by the Nazi regime.

Ignaz Schwarz (1867–1925) was a doctor, antiques dealer, and curator of the first Jewish museum in Vienna. He also published two seminal works, *Das Wiener Ghetto: Seine Häuser und seine Bewohner* (The Vienna Ghetto: its buildings and inhabitants) in 1909 and *Geschichte der Juden in Wien: Von ihrem ersten Auftreten bis zum Jahr 1625* (History of the Jews in Vienna: from its beginnings until 1625) in 1914. Given the

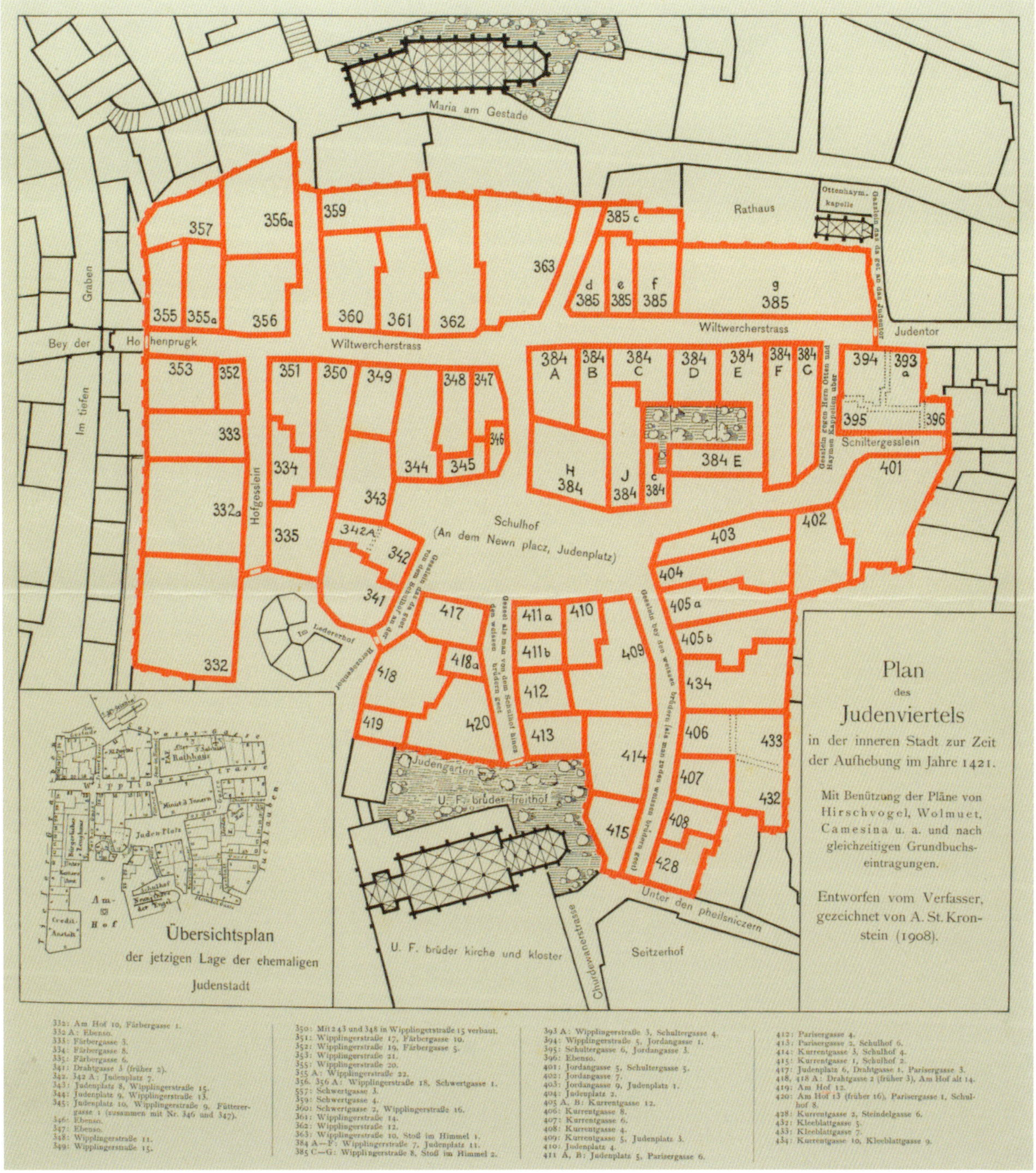

Map dating from 1908, designed by Ignaz Schwarz and drawn by August Stefan Kronstein, showing the Jewish quarter in today's 1st district at the time of its dissolution in 1421; it was based on historical city maps and land register entries.

Hitler Youth on Judenplatz, 1940

knowledge available at the time, Schwarz produced an impressive description of the medieval Jewish quarter, which was not improved upon until the archaeological excavations in the 1990s. **Bernhard Wachstein** (1868–1935) was director of the Library of the Jewish Community of Vienna from 1919 until his death. His genealogical research and two-volume main work, *Die Inschriften des alten Judenfriedhofes in Wien* (Inscriptions of the old Jewish cemetery in Vienna) (1912 and 1917), are of fundamental significance even today in the study of the Jewish history of Vienna. **Samuel Krauss** (1866–1948) taught at the Jewish Theological Institute in Vienna. His 1920 work *Die Wiener Gesera* (The Vienna Gesera) was a pioneering study of the tragic end of the first Jewish community in Vienna. This research reached a wider public in a fictionalized but nevertheless historically accurate form in a 1933 novel by the writer and literary historian Robert Nagel, entitled *Die Juden vom Schulhof: Roman aus der Wiener Judenverfolgung 1421* (The Jews of the Schulhof: Novel about the persecution of the Viennese Jews in 1421). It is more than likely that Nagel knew of the works by Schwarz and Krauss.

For many decades after the Shoah, the official Austrian commemorative culture was dominated by the notion of Austria as "the first victim of National Socialism," which prevailed until well into the 1980s. The monument project in the 1990s paved the way for new pioneering research into the Jewish history of Vienna. The archaeological excavations were the first in Vienna devoted extensively to the Middle Ages rather than Roman times, while the research into the building on Judenplatz 8 was the first of its type whatsoever in Vienna.

The memorial to the Austrian Jewish victims of the Shoah: a Viennese controversy

In the 1980s, widespread discussion arose in German-speaking countries as to an "appropriate" form of public commemoration of the Shoah. Who was to be remembered? Where and in what form (memorials, monuments, figurative or abstract, museums, memorial sites, etc.)? In Austria, this debate began in 1986 in connection with the election of Kurt Waldheim, a former SA officer, as federal president. In the wake of the election, civil society's discussion of Austrian guilt extended beyond the political level to the personal. Around the same time, more and more representatives of the victims of National Socialism also began to call for their own public places of remembrance. This demand was spearheaded in Vienna by Simon Wiesenthal, who for decades had been campaigning for the prosecution of Nazi perpetrators, but also for

Judenplatz 8, c. 1950

Presentation of the winning entry for the design of the Shoah memorial, January 25, 1996; from l. to r.: jury chairman Hans Hollein, the artist Rachel Whiteread, Simon Wiesenthal, and the then mayor of Vienna Michael Häupl

remembrance of the Jewish victims (and those from other groups, such as Roma and Sinti).[7] Wiesenthal's campaign for a memorial to the Jewish victims of the Shoah first attracted wider attention in December 1994, when he publicly criticized Alfred Hrdlicka's memorial against war and fascism on Albertinaplatz, later calling it a "memorial to humiliation."[8] He was referring to the depiction of a Jew washing the sidewalk, which he and many other Jews saw as a continuation of their abasement. Vienna's mayor Michael Häupl immediately agreed to Wiesenthal's call for a separate monument to the Jewish victims of National Socialism. Judenplatz was proposed as the location, not just as a political signal that the memorial was to be located in the center of the city, but also to draw attention to the significance of the site in the city's Jewish history. In January 1996, following an invitation to submit designs, a jury with Wiesenthal and members from Austria and other countries unanimously chose the design by the British sculptor Rachel Whiteread.[9] One condition for the entries was that the designs should not contain any figurative representations. It was left to the entrants' discretion whether they wished to incorporate the excavated remains of the medieval synagogue (only the inscriptions on the monument were predefined). Whiteread's concept was of an inside-out library with the book spines facing inwards, their inaccessibility symbolizing the emptiness and loss of vitality.[10] The memorial allows a variety of interpretations, with frequent reference to Jews as "People of the Book," the significance of this book (the Bible) as a "portable homeland" (Heinrich Heine), and the cultural and intellectual achievements of Austrian Jews before the Shoah. The dimensions of the monument were based on those of the salon in an old Viennese apartment, with a ceiling rosette visible when the memorial is viewed from above. Whiteread's project made no reference to the medieval synagogue, an aspect that led to fierce discussions in the ensuing public debate after the announcement of the jury's decision. The erection of the monument was delayed for several years, before the unveiling finally took place in autumn 2000.[11]

The first protests against the project came from local residents with the support of FPÖ politicians, who complained that the monument would spoil the overall design of the square. In response, a scaffolding mock-up was erected in May 1996 to demonstrate the size and position of the monument.

Much of the political and public debate about the monument revolved around the remains of the medieval synagogue, unearthed until July 1996 by the archaeological excavations, which had turned out to be more extensive than originally planned. The city archaeology department headed by Ortolf Harl had long suspected that excavations on Judenplatz would reveal remnants of the medieval Jewish quarter. The decision to build the monument here provided an opportunity to carry

Scaffolding mock-up of the memorial, 1996

Following double page: The Memorial to the Austrian Jewish Victims of the Shoah; in the background on the right are the Mizrachi House and the entrance to Museum Judenplatz, 2020.

Talente
leben
lernen

MUSEUM
JUDENPLATZ

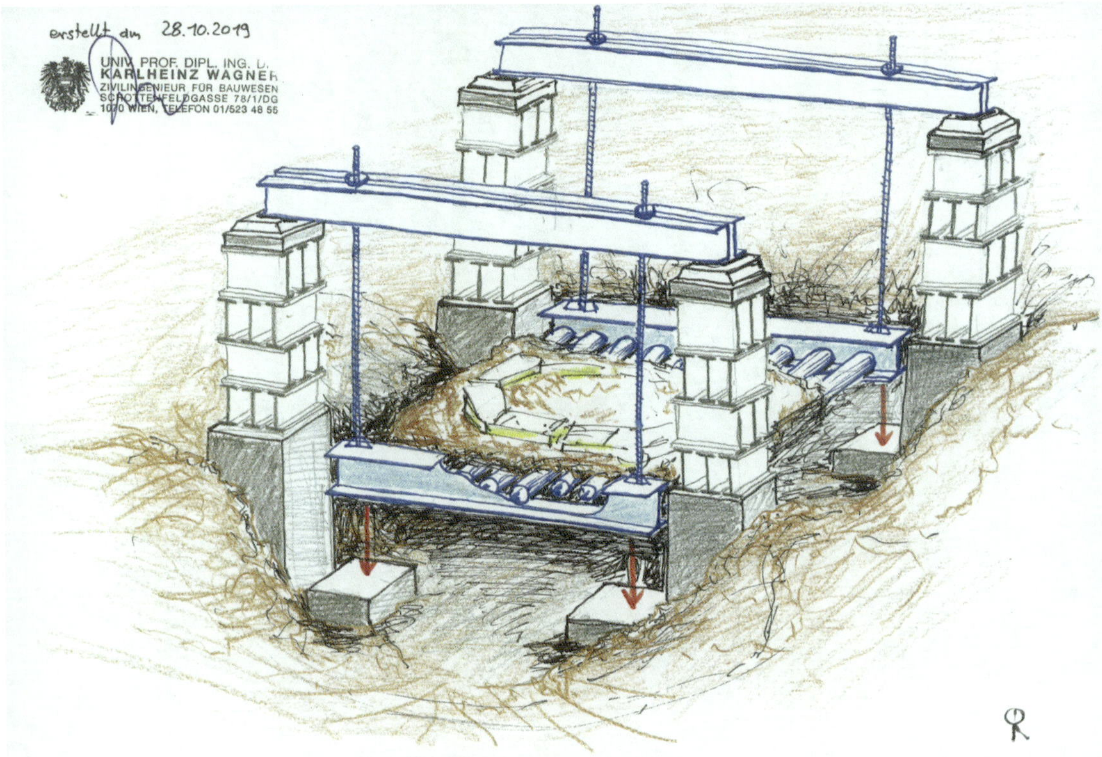

Architectural drawing of the lowering of the bimah, Büro Zivilingenieur Univ.-Prof. DI Dr. Karlheinz Wagner, 2019. The drawing shows how, in 1998, the bimah was moved using a complex construction of steel tubes filled with concrete and four synchronized 100-tonne hydraulic presses.

out these excavations. What the archaeologists eventually discovered far exceeded their expectations. Along with the foundations of the synagogue, they also found the bimah, the central podium from which the Torah was read. This sensational discovery now became the focus of opposition to the memorial project. Prominent representatives of the Jewish Community of Vienna, but also Leon Zelman, head of the Jewish Welcome Service, and the archbishop of Vienna, Cardinal Christoph Schönborn, spoke out against Whiteread's design, stating that the excavations in themselves were a better memorial.[12] Already in the competition brief, parallels had been drawn between the tragic end of the medieval Jewish community and the crimes of the Shoah.[13] However, this linking of the Vienna Gesera with the Shoah in order to highlight the historical continuity of the persecution and murder of Jews runs the risk of likening the two historical and cultural contexts and negating the unique enormity of the Shoah and the completely different dimensions in the number of victims.

Over the years, the memorial project emerged as an opportunity for public and political debate, in which diverse interests, intentions,

Close-up of the bimah in the archaeological display room of Museum Judenplatz, 2020

Unveiling of the Memorial to the Austrian Jewish Victims of the Shoah, October 25, 2000

hopes, and reservations regarding remembrance of the crimes of the Shoah were expressed. Jewish representatives in particular were adamant that responsibility for commemoration did not lie with the victims' descendants, but that the memorial should signify a commitment by society as a whole to the need for remembrance. The memorial should be located in the heart of the city—not on the outskirts, beyond the Danube in the 22nd district, as had been proposed by some critics.

Representatives of the Jewish Community pointed out that although it was not the community's task to push for completion of the project, politicians were increasingly shifting responsibility to it, since the City of Vienna kept postponing the decision on the erection of the monument. The unanswered questions as to whether to locate the memorial on Judenplatz as planned and if so, how to still make the excavations accessible to the public, were effectively left to the Jewish Community to resolve. When rabbis objected to positioning the monument above the bimah, its location was moved by one meter. Moreover, in 1998, the municipal authorities decided that the excavations should be made accessible via an underground passage in Judenplatz 8. To enable the excavations to be displayed, modifications had to be made to the remnants of the synagogue. For structural reasons, only parts of the medieval foundations could be made visible in the exhibition room. In an elaborate and highly complex procedure, the bimah, which weighs around 55 metric tons, was lowered by about 1.5 meters to bring it just slightly above floor level, as it would have been in the medieval synagogue. Without this intervention, only very tall visitors to the underground display room would have been able to see it from above.

The display room and exhibition spaces in the Mizrachi House were designed by Vienna-based architects Jabornegg & Pálffy. The first version of the permanent exhibition (until 2010) contained not only rooms showing the history of Vienna's medieval Jewish community, but also a computer research archive, installed in cooperation with the Documentation Centre of Austrian Resistance (DÖW), with the names and details of 65,000 Austrian Jewish victims of the Shoah.[14] The municipal authorities treated the memorial, excavations, and Museum Judenplatz, a satellite of the Jewish Museum Vienna, as one interlinked Judenplatz remembrance project. Finally, after years of fierce public debate, the memorial was officially unveiled and Museum Judenplatz was able to open on October 25, 2000. The date—the day before the Austrian national holiday—was chosen quite deliberately to underscore the responsibility of all of society for remembering the Shoah.

Endnotes

Danielle Spera
"A contribution in the fight against forgetting"
Judenplatz: a place where past, present, and future come together
→ **pages 6–19**

1 "Austria's delayed Holocaust memorial," BBC News, October 25, 2000.
2 "Ein Beitrag gegen das Vergessen," *Der Standard*, October 24, 2000, p. 2.

Astrid Peterle
Forward from the Present to the Past
The new permanent exhibition at Museum Judenplatz
→ **pages 20–33**

1 Sigrid Czeika, "Der Hund vom Judenplatz—eine archäozoologische Studie," in *Fundort Wien: Berichte zur Archäologie* 3 (2000), Forschungsgesellschaft Wiener Stadtarchäologie, pp. 48–55.
2 See the essay by Siegrid Schmidt in this catalogue, pp. 122–31.

Anna Lidor-Osprian
Vienna's Jewish Community in the Middle Ages
→ **pages 34–45**

1 Eveline Brugger, "Von der Ansiedlung bis zur Vertreibung: Juden in Österreich im Mittelalter," in idem/Martha Keil/Albert Lichtblau/Christoph Lind/Barbara Staudinger, *Geschichte der Juden in Österreich*, 2nd ed. (Vienna, 2013), pp. 123–227, here p. 123.
2 Klaus Lohrmann, *Die Wiener Juden im Mittelalter* (Geschichte der Juden in Wien 1) (Vienna, 2000), p. 22.
3 A good survey of Hebrew sources on the history of the Jews in Austria can be found in Martha Keil, "Gemeinde und Kultur: Die mittelalterlichen Grundlagen jüdischen Lebens in Österreich," in Brugger et al., *Geschichte*, pp. 15–122, here pp. 17–38.
4 For example, for the Vienna community in Paul Mitchell, "Synagoge und jüdische Viertel im mittelalterlichen Wien," in Fritz Backhaus/Egon Warmers, eds., *Synagogen, Mikwen, Siedlungen: Jüdisches Alltagsleben im Lichte neuer archäologischer Funde*, Schriften des Archäologischen Museums Frankfurt 19 (2004), pp. 139–50.
5 Eveline Brugger/Birgit Wiedl, *Regesten zur Geschichte der Juden in Österreich im Mittelalter*, vol.1: *Von den Anfängen bis 1338*, p. 15.
6 Joseph Seemüller, ed., *Österreichische Chronik von den 95 Herrschaften* (MGH Deutsche Chroniken 6) (Hannover, 1909), p. 23.
7 Shlomo Spitzer, *Bne Chet: Die österreichischen Juden im Mittelalter—Eine Sozial- und Kulturgeschichte* (Vienna, 1997), p. 10.
8 Brugger/Wiedl, *Regesten*, p. 15, no. 1; place names containing "Jude(n)" are probably also indications of settlements or places of residence of Jewish merchants along the Danube and other trade routes, see Brugger, "Von der Ansiedlung," p. 125.
9 Report by Ephraim bar Jakob in Adolf Neubauer/Moritz Stern, *Hebräische Berichte über die Judenverfolgungen während der Kreuzzüge* (Quellen zur Geschichte der Juden in Deutschland 2) (Berlin, 1892), p. 74.
10 Brugger/Wiedl, *Regesten*, vol. 1, no. 3, pp. 16–17.
11 Klaus Lohrmann, *Judenrecht und Judenpolitik im mittelalterlichen Österreich* (Handbuch zur Geschichte der Juden in Österreich, Reihe B, 1) (Vienna, 1990), p. 47.
12 Neubauer/Stern, *Berichte*, p. 74 (Hebrew), p. 211 (German).
13 Brugger/Wiedl, *Regesten*, vol. 1, no. 5, pp. 18–19; Brugger, "Ansiedlung," p. 127.
14 Brugger/Wiedl, *Regesten*, vol. 1, nos. 11, 12, pp. 24–25.
15 Ibid., no. 11; Brugger, "Ansiedlung," p. 127.
16 Brugger/Wiedl, *Regesten*, vol. 1, no. 16, pp. 27–28.
17 Transcripts of the first privileges for Viennese Jews in Brugger/Wiedl, *Regesten*, vol. 1, no. 20, pp. 31–32, and no. 25, pp. 35–39; for the development of religious and secular Jewish law, see Lohrmann, *Judenrecht*; Brugger, "Ansiedlung," pp. 130–51.
18 Brugger, "Ansiedlung," p. 140.
19 Seemüller, *95 Herrschaften*, p. 238. The effective protection of the Jews by a ruler was not always viewed favorably by contemporary chroniclers; see comment on "Rintfleisch-Pogrom" in Germany in 1298, ibid., p. 183.
20 On Jewish names in Austria, see Martha Keil, "'Petachja, genannt Zecherl': Namen und Beinamen von Juden im deutschen Sprachraum des Spätmittelalters," in Reinhard Härtel, ed., *Personennamen und Identität*, Grazer grundwissenschaftliche Forschungen, vol. 3 (Schriftenreihe der Akademie Friesach 2) (Graz, 1997), pp. 119–46.
21 Lohrmann, *Wiener Juden*, pp. 111–13.; Moses Ginsburger, "Wien," in Zvi Avneri, ed., *Germania Judaica: Von 1238 zur Mitte des 14. Jahrhunderts*, vol. II/2 (Tübingen, 1968), p. 889; for Jewish migration, see Spitzer, *Bne Chet*, p. 100 n. 2.

22 Brugger, "Ansiedlung," p. 169.
23 Yitzhak Segal/Yosef Schlomo Stefansky, eds., *Meir ben Baruch me-Rothenburg: Sche'elot u-Teschuvot*, vol. 2 (Jerusalem, 2013), p. 15, no. 12.
24 Spitzer, *Bne Chet*, pp. 162–64.
25 Ibid., p. 188.
26 Michael Toch, *Die Juden im mittelalterlichen Reich* (Enzyklopädie deutscher Geschichte 44), 3rd ed. (Munich, 2013), p. 31.
27 Keil, "Gemeinde," pp. 64–68.
28 Martha Keil points out that it is an extended version of an older document from Magdeburg, see Keil, "Geschichte und Kultur," pp. 31–32; for details on traditions, see Spitzer, *Bne Chet*, pp. 201–18.
29 Ibid. pp. 48–49.
30 Spitzer, *Bne Chet*, pp. 130–31.
31 Keil, "Gemeinde," pp. 41–43.
32 Ibid., p. 48.
33 Ibid. pp. 61–64.
34 Spitzer, *Bne Chet*, pp. 124–25; Keil, "Gemeinde," p. 50.
35 Keil, "Gemeinde," p. 50.
36 Spitzer, *Bne Chet*, pp. 126.
37 For the construction phases of the synagogue, see Heidrun Helgert/Martin A. Schmid, "Die mittelalterliche Synagoge auf dem Judenplatz in Wien: Baugeschichte und Rekonstruktion," in Gerhard Milchram, ed., *Wiener Jahrbuch für jüdische Geschichte, Kultur und Museumswesen* 4 (2000), pp. 91–110.
38 Martha Keil, "Bet haKnesset, Judenschul: Die Synagoge als Gotteshaus—Amtsraum und Brennpunkt sozialen Lebens," in Milchram, *Wiener Jahrbuch für jüdische Geschichte, Kultur und Museumswesen* 4 (2000), pp. 71–89, here p. 71.
39 Mitchell, "Synagoge und jüdische Viertel," p. 146.
40 Indications are provided by the gravestone fragments of the medieval cemetery found in the Hofkapelle and elsewhere, see Bernhard Wachstein, *Hebräische Grabsteine aus dem XIII.-XV. Jahrhundert in Wien und Umgebung* (Sitzungsberichte der kaiserlichen Akademie der Wissenschaften 181,1) (Vienna, 1916).
41 Brugger/Wiedl, *Regesten*, vol. 1, no. 25 under point 13, pp. 35–38.
42 Since Ignaz Schwarz, the cemetery is thought to have been located in the area of the Goethe monument near the Hofburg, but further verification is required; see Ignaz Schwarz, *Das Wiener Ghetto, seine Häuser und seine Bewohner* (Quellen und Forschungen zur Geschichte der Juden in Deutsch-Österreich 2) (Vienna, 1909), pp. 53–55.
43 See *Quellen zur Geschichte der Stadt Wien*, dept. III,1, *Grundbücher der Stadt Wien, Die ältesten Kaufbücher* (1368 – 1388), ed. V. Franz Staub (Vienna, 1898), no. 1142.
44 Martha Keil, "Synagoge, Mikwe, Fleischbank: Die mittelalterlichen Judenviertel in Wien und Wiener Neustadt," in *Österreich: Geschichte – Literatur – Geografie* 3 (2016), pp. 265–77, here p. 272.
45 Rudolf Geyer/Leopold Sailer, eds., *Urkunden aus Wiener Grundbüchern zur Geschichte der Wiener Juden im Mittelalter* (Quellen zur Geschichte der Juden in Deutschösterreich 10) (Vienna, 1931), p. 585 no. 1972.
46 Keil, "Synagoge," p. 273.
47 Hartmann Joseph Zeibig, ed., "Kleine Klosterneuburger Chronik: 1322 bis 1428," in *Archiv für Kunde österreichischer Geschichtsquellen* 7 (1851), pp. 227–68, here p. 238.
48 Brugger, "Ansiedlung," pp. 219–21.
49 "Wiener Annalen von 1348-1404," in Seemüller, *95 Herrschaften*, pp. 231–42, here p. 231.
50 Ibid., p. 232.
51 Spitzer, *Bne Chet*, p. 79.
52 Zeibig, "Chronik," pp. 238–39.
53 Johann Egid Scherer, *Die Rechtsverhältnisse der Juden in den deutsch-österreichischen Ländern* (Beiträge zur Geschichte des Judenrechts im Mittelalter 1) (Leipzig, 1901), p. 407.

Paul Mitchell

Judenplatz and the Former Jewish Quarter

Archaeology and building research since 1995

→ pages 46–57

1 Vienna City Archaeology Department, site supervisor Heidrun Helgert, deputy Paul Mitchell; Heidrun Helgert/Martin A. Schmid, "Die mittelalterliche Synagoge auf dem Judenplatz in Wien: Baugeschichte und Rekonstruktion," in Gerhard Milchram, ed., *Wiener Jahrbuch für jüdische Geschichte und Kultur & Museumswesen* 4 (1999/2000), pp. 91–110; idem, "Die mittelalterliche Synagoge auf dem Judenplatz: Verlauf und Ergebnisse des archäologischen Projekts," in *Perspektiven* (2000) 6/7, pp. 47–52; Heidrun Helgert/Paul Mitchell/Martin A. Schmid, "Die mittelalterliche Synagoge auf dem Judenplatz in Wien: Befund – Analogien – Rekonstruktion" (unpublished manuscript), Bibliothek der Stadtarchäologie Wien.
2 A serial number is given to every human activity identified during an excavation (construction of a wall, depositing of material, digging a trench, etc.).
3 Dendrochronology (or tree-ring dating) is the determination of the year a tree was felled by analyzing the tree rings.
4 Led by Paul Mitchell and Doris Schön; Doris Schön, "Von mittelalterlichen Mauern, renaissancezeitlichen Fenstern und barocken Fußböden: Bauforschung im Haus Wien 1, Judenplatz 8," in *Fundort Wien* 6 (2003), pp. 96–141; Paul Mitchell/Doris Schön, "Zur Bauforschung im Misrachihaus: Ein Haus der Judenstadt im Verlauf der Jahrhunderte," in Milchram, *Wiener Jahrbuch für Jüdische Geschichte, Kultur und Museumswesen* 4 (1999/2000), pp. 111–22; idem, "Zu ebener Erde und im ersten Stock: Die Bauforschung der Stadtarchäologie Wien im Misrachi-Haus," in *Perspektiven* (2000) 6/7, pp. 61–64.
5 Structural research by Günther Buchinger, Paul Mitchell, and Doris Schön; excavations by the Vienna City Archaeology Department, mostly led by Martin Mosser; publications too numerous to list here.
6 Ignaz Schwarz, *Das Wiener Ghetto: Seine Häuser und seine Bewohner* (Quellen und Forschungen zur Geschichte der Juden in Deutsch-Österreich 2) (Vienna, 1909); Klaus Lohrmann, *Die Wiener Juden im Mittelalter* (Geschichte der Juden in Wien 1) (Berlin, 2000); Paul Mitchell, "Synagoge und jüdisches Viertel im mittelalterlichen Wien," in Fritz Backhaus/Egon Wamers, eds., *Synagogen, Mikwen,*

Siedlungen Jüdisches Alltagsleben im Lichte neuer archäologischer Funde (Schriften des Archäologischen Museums Frankfurt 19) (Frankfurt, 2004), pp. 139–50; Paul Mitchell, "Topographie und Infrastruktur des Judenviertels im spätmittelalterlichen Wien," in Maria Stürzebecher/Simon Paulus, eds., *Inter Judeos – Topographie und Infrastruktur jüdischer Quartiere im Mittelalter* (Erfurter Schriften zur Jüdischen Geschichte 5) (Erfurt, 2019), pp. 54–63.

7 There was a "Wunderburggasse" in the Jewish quarter in Nuremberg: Lohrmann, p. 101.

Judenplatz 8: A Jewish House with a Varied History
→ pages 60–63

1 For the history of Judenplatz 8, see Doris Schön, pp. 96–139.

2 Thomas Ertl, *Vienna 1448: Steuerwesen und Wohnverhältnisse in einer spätmittelalterlichen Stadt* (Vienna 2020), p. 84.

Eveline Brugger and Birgit Wiedl
Jewish-Christian Cohabitation in Medieval Vienna
→ pages 64–73

* Research for this article was funded by the Austrian Science Fund (FWF): P32395-G28 and P32396-G28.

1 See the overview in Eveline Brugger, "Von der Ansiedlung bis zur Vertreibung: Juden in Österreich im Mittelalter," in idem/Martha Keil/Albert Lichtblau/Christoph Lind/Barbara Staudinger, *Geschichte der Juden in Österreich*, 2nd edn. (Vienna, 2013), pp. 123–227, here pp. 130–51; for details of the 1244 privilege, see Klaus Lohrmann, *Judenrecht und Judenpolitik im mittelalterlichen Österreich* (Vienna, 1990).

2 Martha Keil, "Gemeinde und Kultur – die mittelalterlichen Grundlagen jüdischen Lebens in Österreich," in Brugger/idem/Lichtblau/Lind/Staudinger, pp. 15–122, here pp. 60–72.

3 Eveline Brugger/Birgit Wiedl, *Regesten zur Geschichte der Juden in Österreich im Mittelalter*, vol. 3: 1366–1386, (Innsbruck, 2015), p. 143, no. 1374, 257, no. 1569; Birgit Wiedl, "'... und kam der jud vor mich ze offens gericht': Juden und (städtische) Gerichtsobrigkeiten im Spätmittelalter," in *Mediaevistik: Internationale Zeitschrift für interdisziplinäre Mittelalterforschung* 28 (2016) 2015, pp. 243–68, here pp. 250–52.

4 For examples from the entire Ashkenazic territory, see Joseph Shatzmiller, *Cultural Exchange: Jews, Christians, and Art in the Medieval Marketplace* (Jews, Christians, and Muslims from the Ancient to the Modern World) (Princeton, 2013).

5 Astrid Lembke, ed., *Aventiuren in Aschkenas* (Aschkenas: Zeitschrift für Geschichte und Kultur der Juden 25.1) (Berlin, 2015), pp. 1–160; Martin Przybilski, *Kulturtransfer zwischen Juden und Christen in der deutschen Literatur des Mittelalters* (Quellen und Forschungen zur Literatur- und Kulturgeschichte 61) (Berlin, 2010).

6 Birgit Wiedl, "'Do hiezen si der Juden mesner ruefen': Jüdisch-christliche Geschäftsurkunden als Quellen zur Alltagsgeschichte," in Ludger Lieb/Klaus Oschema/Johannes Heil, eds., *Abrahams Erbe: Konkurrenz, Konflikt und Koexistenz der Religionen im europäischen Mittelalter* (Das Mittelalter: Perspektiven mediävistischer Forschung, supp. 2) (Berlin, 2015), pp. 437–53, here p. 438 and n. 4.

7 Wiedl, *Gerichtsobrigkeiten*, p. 245.

8 For further background on this and on rabbinical considerations, see Michael Toch, *Die Juden im mittelalterlichen Reich* (Enzyklopädie deutscher Geschichte 44), 3rd edn. (Munich, 2013), pp. 40–45.

9 Wiedl, *Geschäftsurkunden*, pp. 437–39.

10 Benjamin Laqua, "Nähe und Distanz: Nachbarrechtliche Regelungen zwischen Christen und Juden (12.–14. Jahrhundert)," in Sigrid Hirbodian/Christian Jörg/Sabine Klapp/Jörg R. Müller, eds., *Pro multis beneficiis: Festschrift für Friedhelm Burgard—Forschungen zur Geschichte der Juden und des Trierer Raums* (Trierer Historische Forschungen 68) (Trier, 2012), pp. 73–92, here pp. 83–85; Gunnar Mikosch, "Zeichen, Bilder: Codes—Prolegomena zu einer Semiotik jüdischer Räume," in Susanne Ehrich/Jörg Oberste, eds., *Städtische Räume im Mittelalter* (Regensburg, 2009), pp. 35–47, here pp. 43–44.

11 Eveline Brugger, "Smoke in the Chapel: Jews and Ecclesiastical Institutions in and around Vienna during the Fourteenth Century," in Philippe Buc/Martha Keil/John Tolan, eds., *Jews and Christians in Medieval Europe: The Historiographical Legacy of Bernhard Blumenkranz* (Religion and Law in Medieval Christian and Muslim Societies 7) (Turnhout, 2016), pp. 79–94, here pp. 88–89.

12 Eveline Brugger/Birgit Wiedl, *Regesten zur Geschichte der Juden in Österreich im Mittelalter*, vol. 2: 1339–1365 (Innsbruck, 2010), pp. 229–32, no. 929.

13 Brugger, *Ansiedlung*, 216–220; Eveline Brugger/Birgit Wiedl, "'Im Haus des Juden fand man eine blutbefleckte Hostie ...' Hostienschändungsvorwürfe und ihre Folgen für die jüdische Bevölkerung Österreichs im Mittelalter," in *Jahrbuch für Landeskunde von Niederösterreich* NF 84 (2018), pp. 35–57, here pp. 46–50.

14 Ignaz Schwarz, *Das Wiener Ghetto, seine Häuser und seine Bewohner* (Quellen und Forschungen zur Geschichte der Juden in Deutsch-Österreich 2) (Vienna, 1909), pp. 136–45.

Martha Keil
Hansüß, Rifka, Joseppin: Women in the Medieval Jewish Quarter
→ pages 78–85

1 Martha Keil, "Hendl, Suessel, Putzlein: Name und Geschlecht am Beispiel des österreichischen Judentums im Spätmittelalter," in *L'Homme: Zeitschrift für feministische Geschichtswissenschaft* 20 (2009) 1, pp. 35-52, here p. 51; an extensive lexicon of medieval Ashkenazi names can be found in Alexander Beider, *A Dictionary of Ashkenazic Given Names: Their Origins, Structure, Pronunciation, and Migrations* (Bergenfield, NJ, 2001).

2 Martha Keil, "'Petachja, genannt Zecherl': Namen und Beinamen von Juden im deutschen Sprachraum des Spätmittelalters," in Reinhard Härtel, ed., *Personennamen und Identität* (Grazer grundwissenschaftliche Forschungen),

vol. 3, Schriftenreihe der Akademie Friesach 2 (Graz, 1997), pp. 119–46, here pp. 120–21.

3 Keil, "Hendl", p. 43.

4 See Klaus Lohrmann, *Die Wiener Juden im Mittelalter* (Berlin/Vienna, 2000), pp. 115, 136.

5 Martha Keil, "Unsichtbare Frauen oder '…was nicht sein darf': Jüdische Geschäftsfrauen im Spätmittelalter als Forschungsobjekte," in Gabriele Kohlbauer-Fritz, ed., *Beste aller Frauen: Weibliche Dimensionen im Judentum*, exh. cat, Jewish Museum Vienna (June 2007), pp. 99–107; Martin Dolch, "Rose Welen, eine Jüdin in Kaiserslautern: Analyse der Urkunde von 1344 Januar 2," in *Pfälzer Heimat* 47 (1996), pp. 98–100.

6 Michael Toch, "Die jüdische Frau im Erwerbsleben des Spätmittelalters," in Julius Carlebach, ed., *Zur Geschichte der jüdischen Frau in Deutschland* (Berlin, 1993), pp. 37–48, here p. 37.

7 Österreichisches Staatsarchiv, Finanz- und Hofkammerarchiv, Alte Hofkammer, Vizedomamt Urbare 1067B, Artur Goldmann, ed., *Das Judenbuch der Scheffstrasse zu Wien (1389–1420), mit einer Schriftprobe* (Vienna, 1908).

8 Lohrmann, *Die Wiener Juden*, pp. 127–34; Martha Keil, "'Maistrin' und Geschäftsfrau: Jüdische Oberschichtfrauen im spätmittelalterlichen Österreich," in Sabine Hödl, idem, eds., *Die jüdische Familie in Geschichte und Gegenwart* (Berlin-Bodenheim, 1999), pp. 27–50, here pp. 39–43.

9 Goldmann, *Das Judenbuch*, XL–XLII; Martha Keil, "Geschäftserfolg und Steuerschulden: Jüdische Frauen in österreichischen Städten des Spätmittelalters," in Günther Hödl/Fritz Mayrhofer/Ferdinand Opll, eds., *Frauen in der Stadt* (Beiträge zur Geschichte der Städte Mitteleuropas, vol. 18) = Schriftenreihe der Akademie Friesach 7 (Linz, 2003), pp. 37–62, here pp. 38–39. The figures were adjusted in accordance with the Jewish document registers published in 2003, http://www.injoest.ac.at/de/downloads/buecher (accessed on Dec 15, 2019).

10 Eveline Brugger, "Von der Ansiedlung bis zur Vertreibung: Juden in Österreich im Mittelalter," in idem, Martha Keil, Christoph Lind, et al., *Geschichte der Juden in Österreich*, 2nd edition (Vienna, 2013), pp. 123–227, here p. 220 (Salzburg 1404), p. 223 (imprisonment 1420).

11 Martha Keil, "What happened to the 'New Christians'? The 'Viennese Geserah' of 1420/21 and the forced baptism of the Jews," in Philippe Buc/idem/John Tolan, eds., *Jews and Christians in Medieval Europe: The Historiographical Legacy of Bernhard Blumenkranz* (Religion and Law in Medieval Christian and Muslim Societies 7) (Turnhout, 2016), pp. 97 –114, here pp. 102–3.

12 Martha Keil, "Mobilität und Sittsamkeit: Jüdische Frauen im Wirtschaftsleben des spätmittelalterlichen Aschkenas," in Michael Toch, ed., *Wirtschaftsgeschichte der mittelalterlichen Juden: Fragen und Einschätzungen* (Schriften des Historischen Kollegs München, Kolloquien 71) (Munich, 2008), pp. 153–80, here pp. 157–66.

13 Eveline Brugger/Birgit Wiedl, *Regesten zur Geschichte der Juden in Österreich im Mittelalter*, vol. 1: Von den Anfängen bis 1338 (Innsbruck, 2005), p. 69, no. 53 (1275 XI 12, Vienna); Keil, "Maistrin", p. 27; Klaus Lohrmann, "Gemeinde – Haus – Familie: Die Bedeutung der Familie in der jüdischen Gemeinde des Mittelalters," in Hödl/Keil, eds., pp. 9–26, here pp. 15–18.

14 Brugger/Wiedl, *Regesten* 1, p. 228, no. 260 (1324 III 25, Vienna: Hendlein); Eveline Brugger/Birgit Wiedl, *Regesten zur Geschichte der Juden in Österreich im Mittelalter*, vol. 2: 1339–1365 (Innsbruck, 2010), p. 84, no. 619 (1348 VIII 13, Vienna: Rötlein); p. 149, no. 759 (1353 XII 13, Vienna: Haeschlein).

15 Brugger/Wiedl, *Regesten 2*, p. 14, no. 465 (1339 VII 24, Vienna); for details of other loans, see the entry for "Plume" in the register in idem, *Regesten* 1, p. 432, and idem, *Regesten* 2, p. 418.

16 Keil, "Maistrin", pp. 39–43.

17 HHStA, Allgemeine Urkundenreihe (AUR) 1477 IX 15 and 1479 II 12; Keil, "Mobilität", pp. 162–63.

18 See Pierre Bourdieu, "Ökonomisches Kapital, kulturelles Kapital, soziales Kapital," in Reinhard Kreckel, ed., *Soziale Ungleichheiten: Soziale Welt* (Göttingen, 1983), pp. 183–98.

19 Lohrmann, *Die Wiener Juden*, pp. 127–30; Brugger/Wiedl, *Regesten* 1, p. 188, no. 193 (1314 VIII 10, Vienna); for details of business transactions after Lebman's death, see Eveline Brugger, "Loans of the Father: Business Succession in Families of Jewish Moneylenders in Late Medieval Austria," in Finn-Einar Eliassen/Katalin Szende, eds., *Generations in Towns: Succession and Success in Pre-Industrial Urban Societies* (Newcastle upon Tyne, 2009), pp. 112–29, here pp. 114–15.

Who Wrote Manuscripts in the Middle Ages? Hannah bat Menahem: An Example of a Female Scribe
→ pages 88–89

1 Colette Sirat, "Hannah bat Menahem Zion finished her copy of the Sefer Mitzwot Qatan," in Adri K. Offenberg/Emile G. L. Schrijver/Frits J. Hoogewoud, *Bibliotheca Rosenthaliana: Treasures of Jewish Booklore* (Amsterdam, 1994), p. 7.

Thomas Kühtreiber

May the Impure Serve to Clean

A late medieval jug in the form of a Jew, found in Krems an der Donau
→ pages 90–97

1 museumkrems, inv. no. H1235. Pictures of the object taken from all angles can be found at https://realonline.imareal.sbg.ac.at/detail/?archivnr=004799 (accessed on March 30, 2020). For publications to date, see Leopold Schmidt, "Volkskunde der Gotischen Epochen," in Fritz Dworschak/Harry Kühnel, eds., *Die Gotik in Niederösterreich: Kunst, Kultur und Geschichte eines Landes im Spätmittelalter*, exh. cat., Krems an der Donau (Vienna, 1963), pp. 214–21, here p. 215; Gerhard Jaritz, "Fragment eines Aquamaniles in der Gestalt eines Juden," in Herwig Wolfram/Karl Brunner/Gottfried Stangler, eds., *Die Kuenringer: Das Werden des Landes Niederösterreich*, exh. cat., Niederösterreichische Landesausstellung, Stift Zwettl, May 16 – October 26, 1981, *Kataloge des Niederösterreichischen Landesmuseums*, N.F. 110 (Vienna, 1981), p. 122, cat. no. 117.

2 Sara Lipton, *Dark Mirror—The Medieval Origins of Anti-Jewish Iconography* (New York, 2014).

3 For example, Herbert Hoffmann, *Attic Red-Figured Rhyta* (Mainz, 1962); idem, *Tarentine Rhyta* (Mainz, 1966); Susanne Elbinghaus, "Between Greece and Persia: Rhyta in Thrace from the Late 5th to the Early 3rd Centuries B.C.," in Gocha R. Tsetskhladze, ed., *Ancient Greeks West and East* (Leiden, 1999), pp. 385–425; Robert B. Koehl, *Aegean Bronze Age Rhyta (Prehistory Monographs)* 19 (Philadelphia, 2006).
4 Most recently, Peter Barnet/Peter Dandridge, eds., *Lions, Dragons and Other Beasts: Aquamanilia of the Middle Ages—Vessels for Church and Table*, exh. cat. (New York, New Haven/London, 2006); Joanna Olchawa, *Aquamanilien: Genese, Verbreitung und Bedeutung in islamischen und christlichen Zeremonien* (Bronzegeräte des Mittelalters 8) (Regensburg, 2019), pp. 73–78.
5 Ibid., pp. 143–77.
6 For example, Eberhard Kasten, "Tönerne figürliche Gießgefäße des Mittelalters in Mitteleuropa," in *Arbeits- und Forschungsberichte zur sächsischen Bodendenkmalpflege* 20/21 (1976), pp. 387–558; Hans-Georg Stephan, "Aquamanilien—Figürliche Gießgefäße aus Keramik: Typologie, Chronologie, Gedanken zu Funktion, Verbreitung und Materialität eines mittelalterlichen Tafelgeräts und Statussymbols," in Rainer Atzbach/Patrick Cassitti/Hauke Kenzler/Luitgard Löw, eds., *Archäologie Mittelalter—Neuzeit—Zukunft: Festschrift für Ingolf Ericsson* (Bamberger Schriften zur Archäologie des Mittelalters und der Neuzeit 6) (Bonn, 2017), pp. 521–68.
7 For example, Anna-Elisabeth Theuerkauff-Liederwald, *Mittelalterliche Bronze- und Messinggefäße: Eimer, Kannen, Lavabo-Kessel* (Bronzegeräte Mitteleuropas 4) (Berlin, 1988); Elfriede Hannelore Huber, "Spielen mit der Form: Bügelkannen mit zoomorphen Ausgussröhren aus dem keramischen Fundgut Wiens," in *Beiträge zur Mittelalterarchäologie in Österreich* 27 (2011), pp. 91–101.
8 See Ulrich Müller, *Zwischen Gebrauch und Bedeutung: Studien zur Funktion von Sachkultur am Beispiel mittelalterlichen Handwaschgeschirrs (5./6. bis 15./16. Jahrhundert)* (Zeitschrift für Archäologie des Mittelalters, supplement 20) (Bonn, 2006); Olchawa, *Aquamanilien*, pp. 179–92.
9 Müller, *Gebrauch*, pp. 272–78.
10 Olchawa, *Aquamanilien*, pp. 24–27.
11 Meinolf Schumacher, "'Lavabo in innocentia manus meas ...' Zwischen Schuldanerkennung und Schuldabwehr: Händewaschen im christlichen Kult," in Robert Jütte/Romedio Schmitz-Esser, eds., *Handgebrauch: Geschichten von der Hand aus dem Mittelalter und der Frühen Neuzeit* (Paderborn, 2019), pp. 59–77, here pp. 65–66.
12 Olchawa, *Aquamanilien*, p. 24.
13 For hand-washing rituals in the Christian Catholic mass and the use of aquamaniles, see Olchawa, *Aquamanilien*, pp. 184–86; Schumacher, *Lavabo*, pp. 67–68, 72–75.
14 Robert Jütte, "Hand washing before meals – a distinctive marker between Jews and Gentiles before the Emancipation," in Jütte/Schmitz-Esser, pp. 97–110, here p. 98 (with bibliography).
15 Joanna Olchawa, "Aquamanilien und ihr Gebrauch in islamischen, christlichen und jüdischen Handwaschungsriten," in Jütte/Schmitz-Esser, pp. 39–57, here pp. 55–56.
16 Quoted in Peter Barnet, "Medieval Lion Aquamanilia with Hebrew Inscriptions," in *Images* 3 (2009), pp. 29-37, here p. 34 (will illustration).
17 "Baruch ata ado-nai, elohenu melech ha-olam asher kideshanu bemitzvotav, vetzivanu 'al netilat "yadayim," quoted in Jütte, "Hand washing," p. 102; on the extended blessing, see also Johannes Reiss, "Über das Waschen der Hände," in Wolfgang Gürtler/Gerhard Winkler, eds., *Forscher—Gestalter—Vermittler: Festschrift Gerald Schlag* (Wissenschaftliche Arbeiten aus dem Burgenland) (Eisenstadt, 2001), pp. 357–61 (also with an illustration of a hand-washing vessel from 1910 with the same blessing); the blessing was also recited later during cleansing rituals after menstruation or giving birth (my thanks to Martha Keil for this information).
18 Olchawa, *Aquamanilien*, pp. 143–75.
19 See, e.g., Debra Hassig, "Sex in the Bestiaries," in idem, ed., *The Mark of the Beast: The Medieval Bestiary in Art, Life and Literature* (New York, 1999), pp. 71–98; Birgit Wiedl, "Laughing at the Beast: The Judensau: Anti-Jewish Propaganda and Humor from the Middle Ages and Early Modern Period," in Albrecht Classen, ed., *Laughter in the Middle Ages and Early Modern Times* (Fundamentals of Medieval and Early Modern Culture 5) (Berlin/New York, 2010), pp. 325–64, here pp. 327, 329–31.
20 Olchawa, *Aquamanilien*, pp. 153, 472–75.

Nora Berend

Anti-Jewish Stereotypes from the Middle Ages until Today

→ pages 112–21

1 The form "anti-Semitism" suggests there is a "Semitism" one can oppose, and hence reinforces antisemite stereotypes.
2 Salo W. Baron, "Newer Emphases in Jewish History," *Jewish Social Studies* 25, no. 4 (1963), pp. 245–58; reprinted in his *History and Jewish Historians: Essays and Addresses* (Philadelphia, 1964), pp. 90–106, here p. 96. For a recent critical analysis: Adam Teller, "Revisiting Baron's "Lachrymose Conception": The Meanings of Violence in Jewish History," *AJS Review* 38, no. 2 (2014), pp. 431–39.
3 Steven Beller, *Antisemitism: A Very Short Introduction*, 2nd ed. (Oxford, 2015).
4 Walter Laqueur, *The Changing Face of Anti-Semitism: From Ancient Times to the Present Day* (Oxford, 2006).
5 Gavin I. Langmuir, *Toward a Definition of Antisemitism* (Berkeley, 1996), pp. 301–02.
6 *Ibid.*, pp. 302, 306.
7 Yosef H. Yerushalmi, *Assimilation and Racial Anti-Semitism: The Iberian and the German Models*, Leo Baeck Memorial Lecture 26 (New York, 1982).
8 Rainer Walz, "Der vormoderne Antisemitismus: Religiöser Fanatismus oder Rassenwahn?" *Historische Zeitschrift* 260, no. 3 (1995), pp. 719–48.
9 David Nirenberg, *Anti-Judaism: The Western Tradition* (New York, 2013).
10 Sara Lipton, *Dark Mirror: The Medieval Origins of Anti-Jewish Iconography* (New York, 2014), p. 9.

11 Robert Chazan, *Medieval Stereotypes and Modern Antisemitism* (Berkeley, 1997); Jonathan Adams, Cordelia Heß, eds., *The Medieval Roots of Antisemitism: Continuities and Discontinuities from the Middle Ages to the Present Day* (New York, 2018).
12 Thomas Sizgorich, *Violence and Belief in Late Antiquity: Militant Devotion in Christianity and Islam* (Philadelphia, 2009).
13 Robert Chazan, *From Anti-Judaism to Anti-Semitism: Ancient and Medieval Christian Constructions of Jewish History* (Cambridge, 2016); Robert Chazan, *The Jews of Medieval Western Christendom 1000–1500* (Cambridge, 2009); Anna Sapir Abulafia, *Christian-Jewish Relations 1000–1300: Jews in the Service of Medieval Christendom* (Harlow, 2011).
14 Anna Sapir Abulafia, *Christians and Jews in Dispute: Disputational Literature and the Rise of Anti-Judaism in the West (c. 1000-1150)* (Aldershot, 1998); Jonathan Adams and Jussi Hanska, eds., *The Jewish–Christian Encounter in Medieval Preaching* (London, 2015). See also Juliette Braillon-Philippe, ed., *Le juif errant: un témoin du temps* (Paris, 2001).
15 Emily M. Rose, *The Murder of William of Norwich: The Origins of the Blood Libel in Medieval Europe* (Oxford, 2015); Irven M. Resnick, "Medieval Roots of the Myth of Jewish Male Menses," *The Harvard Theological Review* 93, no. 3 (2000), pp. 241–63.
16 Po-chia Hsia, *Trent 1475: Stories of a Ritual Murder Trial* (New Haven, 1992).
17 Joseph Shatzmiller, *Shylock Reconsidered: Jews, Moneylending and Medieval Society* (Berkeley, 1990).
18 Malcolm C. Barber, "Lepers, Jews and Moslems: The Plot to Overthrow Christendom in 1321," in *History: The Journal of the Historical Association* 66 (1981), pp. 1–17; Norman Roth, "The Jews and the Muslim Conquest of Spain," in *Jewish Social Studies* 38, no. 2 (1976), pp. 145–58; François Soyer, *Antisemitic Conspiracy Theories in the Early Modern Iberian World: Narratives of Fear and Hatred* (Leiden, 2019).
19 Lipton, *Dark Mirror*, pp. 107–08, pp. 172–82.

Siegrid Schmidt

From *Der kleine Ritter Trenk* to *Game of Thrones*

The Middle Ages for all age groups

→ **pages 122–31**

1 Cover blurb of Guido Wandrey, *Mein kleiner Wimmelspass: Ritter* (Stuttgart, 2019).
2 Kirsten Boie, *Der kleine Ritter Trenk* (Hamburg, 2016); Christina Björk/Eva Eriksson, *Sieben kleine Ritter und jede Menge Drachen* (Hamburg, 2015).
3 Auguste Lechner, *Die Nibelungen*, 8th ed. (Innsbruck, 1981).
4 Ibid., pp. 31, 57.
5 For example, stories in *Der kleine Ritter Trenk* about Trenk's little sister Mia-Mina (e.g., p. 188) and his girlfriend Thekla (pp. 82ff.).
6 Martin Grzimek, *Tristan, Roman um Treue, Liebe und Verrat* (Munich, 2011).
7 Noah Gordon, *The Physician*, (New York, 1986), filmed as *Der Medicus* by Philipp Stölzl in 2012.
8 Katharina Zeppezauer-Wachauer, *Kurzwîl als Entertainment: Das Mittelalterfest als popkulturelle Mittelalterrezeption* (Marburg, 2012), esp. pp. 17–18.
9 Tankred Dorst/Ursula Ehler, *Merlin oder Das wüste Land* (Frankfurt am Main, 1981); Christoph Hein, *Die Ritter der Tafelrunde, Eine Komödie* (Berlin, 1990).

Domagoj Akrap

From "Kammergut" to "Hofbefreiung"

Jews in Vienna in the early modern era

→ **pages 132–45**

1 HHStA RK Reichsregister M fol. 11v.
2 Jana Madlen Schütte, *Medizin im Konflikt, Fakultäten, Märkte und Experten in deutschen Universitätsstädten des 14. bis 16. Jahrhunderts (Education and Society in the Middle Ages and Renaissance* p. 53) (Leiden, 2017), p. 299.
3 Ignaz Schwarz, *Geschichte der Juden in Wien bis zum Jahre 1625* (Vienna, 1913), p. 46, n. 7.
4 Schütte, pp. 329–78.
5 Jörg R. Müller, "Maximilian I. und die Juden—Schlaglichter," in *"Vor halbtausend Jahren ..." Festschrift zur Erinnerung an den Besuch des Kaisers Maximilian I. in St. Wendel* (St. Wendel, 2012), p. 87.
6 Peter Rauscher, ed., *Austria Judaica, Quellen zur Geschichte der Juden in Niederösterreich und Wien 1496–1671* (Quelleneditionen des Instituts für Österreichische Geschichtsforschung 7) (Vienna, 2011), pp. 221–22.
7 A. F. Pribram, *Urkunden und Akten zur Geschichte der Juden in Wien, erste Abteilung, allgemeiner Teil 1526–1847* (1849) (Quellen und Forschungen zur Geschichte der Juden in Deutsch-Österreich VIII) (Vienna/Leipzig, 1918) , pp. 1–5.
8 Barbara Staudinger, "Von Silberhändlern und Münzjuden," in *David* 68, April 2006, pp. 28–31.
9 Barbara Staudinger, "Die Zeit der Landjuden und der Wiener Judenstadt 1496-1670/71," in Eveline Brugger/Martha Keil/Albert Lichtblau/Christoph Lind/idem, *Geschichte der Juden in Österreich* (Herwig Wolfram, ed., *Österreichische Geschichte*) (Vienna, 2006), p. 251.
10 Bernhard Wachstein, *Die Inschriften des alten Judenfriedhofes in Wien*, 2 vols. (Vienna, 1912 and 1917); Traude Veran, *Das steinerne Archiv, der alte Judenfriedhof in der Rossau* (Vienna, 2002).
11 Sabine Hödl, "Zur Geschichte der Juden in Österreich unter der Enns 1550–1625," diss., University of Vienna 1998, p. 136.
12 Pribram, p. 79.
13 "Interim auch die Juden sich / Etwas erzaigten ghorsamlich, / Vnterm Lubegg nemblich zur frist / (Wos Haus bey der gulden Gans ist) / In schön Priesterlichem Ornat, / Mit ihrm Talmuth vnd zehn Gebott, / Sambt einem Himel, so mit Zier / Formiert vnd gmacht nach ihr Monier." Johann Holzmüller, "Königklicher Eintritt vnd Empfang," in Albert Camesina, *Beschreibung des feierlichen Einzuges des Königs Matthias in die Stadt Wien im Jahre 1608* [Vienna, 1866], p. 127. Camesina's book also contains a second source, a report by Hieronymus Ortelius, which also mentions the homage paid to Matthias by the Jews.
14 Hödl, p. 45.

15 Ibid., p. 139.
16 Rauscher, p. 67.
17 Ibid., pp. 187–89.
18 Arthur Zacharias Schwarz, "Aus der Briefsammlung Sebastian Tengnagels," in *Zeitschrift für hebräische Bibliographie* 20 (1917), pp. 74–75.
19 Alfred Landau/Bernhard Wachstein, *Jüdische Privatbriefe aus dem Jahre 1619* (Quellen und Forschungen zur Geschichte der Juden in Deutsch-Österreich III) (Vienna, 1911), pp. 4–6; Peter Trawnicek, *Münzjuden unter Ferdinand II. nach den Akten des Hofkammerarchivs in Wien* (Kiel, 2010), pp. 340–41.
20 Wachstein (see note 10), vol. 1, pp. 216–17.

The Lessing Monument on Judenplatz: A Story from the Turbulent Twentieth Century
→ pages 150–51

1 "Die Enthüllung des Lessing-Denkmals," in *Der Wiener Tag*, June 16, 1935, p. 3.

Astrid Peterle
Judenplatz
Biography of an urban space
→ pages 152–67

1 Heidrun Helgert/Martin A. Schmid, "Die mittelalterliche Synagoge auf dem Judenplatz in Wien: Baugeschichte und Rekonstruktion," in Gerhard Milchram for the Jewish Museum Vienna, ed., *Über das Mittelalter: Wiener Jahrbuch für jüdische Geschichte, Kultur & Museumswesen*, vol. 4 (1999/2000), pp. 103–04.
2 Richard Perger, *Straßen, Türme und Basteien: Das Straßennetz der Wiener City in seiner Entwicklung und seinen Namen—Ein Handbuch: Forschungen und Beiträge zur Wiener Stadtgeschichte*, vol. 22 (Vienna, 1991), p. 71.
3 Theodor Georg von Karajan, ed., *Michael Beheim's Buch von den Wienern 1462–1465* (Vienna, 1843), p. 243, line 13.
4 Doris Schön, "Von spätmittelalterlichen Mauern, renaissancezeitlichen Fenstern und barocken Fußböden: Bauforschung im Haus Wien 1, Judenplatz 8," in *Fundort Wien: Berichte zur Archäologie* 6 (2003), Forschungsgesellschaft Wiener Stadtarchäologie, p. 109.
5 Reinhard Pohanka, "Der Judenplatz nach 1421," in *Perspektiven* no. 6/7 (2000), p. 37; various market plans in WStLA, e.g., inv. no. 3.2.1.1.P1.371.2.
6 Johann Evangelist Schlager, *Wiener Skizzen aus dem Mittelalter* (Vienna, 1839), pp. 359ff.
7 For Simon Wiesenthal's contribution to the erection of the monument, see Astrid Peterle, "'Ein Denkmal, das dem Verständnis von uns Juden entspricht ...': Simon Wiesenthal und das Mahnmal für die österreichischen jüdischen Opfer der Schoa am Wiener Judenplatz," in *Wiesenthal in Wien*, exh. cat., Jewish Museum Vienna (Vienna, 2015), pp. 97–101.
8 "Immer öfter die Frage nach dem Großvater," in *Die Presse*, December 21, 1994, p. 3; Wiesenthal speaks of a "memorial to humiliation and intolerance" in his essay "On the History of Jews in Austria," in Kunsthalle Wien, ed., *Judenplatz Wien 1996: Competition Monument and Memorial Site dedicated to the Jewish victims of the Nazi Regime in Austria 1938-1945*, exh. cat., Kunsthalle Vienna (Vienna, 1996) p. 100.
9 See ibid. for details of the competition and the submissions by the invited artists.
10 For details on the numerous academic discussions about Whiteread's monument and the whole project of the redesign of Judenplatz and Museum Judenplatz, see, e.g., Mechtild Widrich, "The Willed and the Unwilled Monument: Judenplatz Vienna and Riegl's *Denkmalpflege*," in *Journal of the Society of Architectural Historians*, vol. 72, no. 3 (September 2013), pp. 382–98; and Barbara Schröder/Monika Sommer, "An On-going Memory? Das Mahnmal für die ermordeten Juden Österreichs revisited," in *zeitgeschichte* 5 (2004), pp. 302–14.
11 For a comprehensive overview of the evolution of the project and the associated controversy and debate, see Simon Wiesenthal, ed., *Projekt: Judenplatz Wien—Zur Konstruktion von Erinnerung* (Vienna, 2000); also *Perspektiven* 6/7 (2000) and Gerhard Milchram, ed., *Judenplatz: Ort der Erinnerung* (Vienna, 2000).
12 See "Die Steine am Judenplatz," in *Berliner Zeitung*, July 22, 2007; "Lasst die Ausgrabungen sprechen," in APA, August 8, 1996; "'Mischt sich in Juden-Diskussion ein': Schönborn lässt Wogen hochgehen," in *Die Presse*, November 21, 1997, p. 12.
13 See various essays in Kunsthalle Wien, ed., *Judenplatz* (Vienna, 1996).
14 The database is now searchable online at: https://www.doew.at/personensuche (accessed on May 11, 2020).

Selected bibliography

Adams, Jonathan and Cordelia Heß, eds. *The Medieval Roots of Antisemitism: Continuities and Discontinuities from the Middle Ages to the Present Day*. New York, 2018.

Avneri, Zvi, ed. *Germania Judaica: Von 1238 zur Mitte des 14. Jahrhunderts*. Vol. 1, *Aachen – Luzern* and vol. 2, *Maastricht – Zwolle*. Tübingen, 1968.

Beinart, Haim. *Geschichte der Juden: Atlas der Verfolgung und Vertreibung im Mittelalter*. Augsburg, 1998.

Beller, Steven. *Antisemitism: A Very Short Introduction*. 2nd ed. Oxford, 2015.

Berend, Nora. *At the Gate of Christendom: Jews, Muslims and 'Pagans' in Medieval Hungary, c. 1000–c. 1300*. Cambridge, 2001.

Brugger, Eveline, Martha Keil, Albert Lichtblau, Christoph Lind, and Barbara Staudinger. *Geschichte der Juden in Österreich*. Österreichische Geschichte, edited by Herwig Wolfram, vol. 15. Vienna, 2006.

Brugger, Eveline and Birgit Wiedl, eds. *Ein Thema—zwei Perspektiven: Juden und Christen in Mittelalter und Frühneuzeit*. Innsbruck, 2007.

Brugger, Eveline and Birgit Wiedl. *Regesten zur Geschichte der Juden in Österreich im Mittelalter*. Vol. 1, *Von den Anfängen bis 1338*. Edited by the Institute for Jewish History in Austria. Innsbruck, 2005.

Brugger, Eveline and Birgit Wiedl. *Regesten zur Geschichte der Juden in Österreich im Mittelalter*. Vol. 2, *1339–1365*. Edited by the Institute for Jewish History in Austria. Innsbruck, 2010.

Brugger, Eveline and Birgit Wiedl. *Regesten zur Geschichte der Juden in Österreich im Mittelalter*. Vol. 3, *1366–1386*. Edited by the Institute for Jewish History in Austria. Innsbruck, 2015.

Brugger, Eveline and Birgit Wiedl. *Regesten zur Geschichte der Juden in Österreich im Mittelalter*. Vol. 4, *1387–1404*. Edited by the Institute for Jewish History in Austria. Innsbruck, 2018.

Burgard, Friedhelm, Alfred Haverkamp, and Gerd Mentgen, eds. *Judenvertreibungen in Mittelalter und früher Neuzeit*. Forschungen zur Geschichte der Juden, Abteilung A, Abhandlungen, vol. 9. Hannover, 1999.

Chazan, Robert. *From Anti-Judaism to Anti-Semitism: Ancient and Medieval Christian Constructions of Jewish History*. Cambridge, 2016.

Clemens, Lukas and Christoph Cluse, eds. *The Jews of Europe around 1400: Disruption, Crisis, and Resilience*. Wiesbaden, 2018.

Cohen, Mark R. *Unter Kreuz und Halbmond: Die Juden im Mittelalter*. Munich, 2005.

Czeika, Sigrid. "Der Hund vom Judenplatz—eine archäozoologische Studie." In vol. 3 of *Fundort Wien: Berichte zur Archäologie*, 48–55. Vienna, 2000.

Doležalová, Eva. *Juden in der mittelalterlichen Stadt: Der städtische Raum im Mittelalter—Ort des Zusammenlebens und des Konflikts*. Prague, 2015.

Eidelberg, Shlomo. *Jewish Life in Austria in the XVth Century as Reflected in the Legal Writings of Rabbi Israel Isserlein and His Contemporaries*. Philadelphia, 1962.

Elbel, Petr and Wolfram Ziegler. "*Am schwarczen suntag mardert man dieselben juden, all die zaigten vill guets an under der erden...* Die Wiener Gesera: eine Neubetrachtung." In *"Avigdor, Benesch, Gitl": Juden in Böhmen, Mähren und Schlesien im Mittelalter—Samuel Steinherz zum Gedenken (1857 Güssing–1942 Theresienstadt)*, edited by Helmut Teufel, Pavel Kocman, and Milan Řepa, 201–68. Brno, 2016.

Geyer, Rudolf and Leopold Sailer, eds. *Urkunden aus Wiener Grundbüchern zur Geschichte der Wiener Juden im Mittelalter*. Quellen und Forschungen zur Geschichte der Juden in Deutsch-Österreich, vol. 10. Vienna, 1931.

Goldmann, Artur. *Das Judenbuch der Scheffstrasse zu Wien (1389–1420)*. Quellen und Forschungen zur Geschichte der Juden in Deutsch-Österreich, vol. 1. Vienna, 1908.

Groebner, Valentin. *Das Mittelalter hört nicht auf: Über historisches Erzählen*. Munich, 2008.

Grossman, Avraham. *Pious and Rebellious: Jewish Women in Medieval Europe*. Hannover, 2004.

Gruber, Elisabeth, Christina Lutter, and Oliver Jens Schmitt, eds. *Kulturgeschichte der Überlieferung im Mittelalter: Quellen und Methoden zur Geschichte Mittel- und Südosteuropas.* Vienna, 2017.

Haverkamp-Rott, Eva. "Jüdische Münzmeister und ihre Münzen im Kontext von Handel und Geldhandel." In *Geprägte Bilderwelten der Romanik: Münzkunst und Währungsräume zwischen Brixen und Prag.* Runkelsteiner Schriften zur Kulturgeschichte, edited by Stiftung Bozner Schlösser, vol. 11, 155–91. Bolzano, 2017.

Helgert, Heidrun and Aartin A. Schmid. "Die mittelalterliche Synagoge auf dem Judenplatz: Verlauf und Ergebnisse des archäologischen Projekts." *Perspektiven* 6/7 (2000), 47–52.

Hödl, Sabine. "Zur Geschichte der Juden in Österreich unter der Enns 1550–1625." PhD diss., University of Vienna, 1998.

Hödl, Sabine and Martha Keil, eds. *Die jüdische Familie in Geschichte und Gegenwart.* Berlin, 1999.

Hödl, Sabine, Peter Rauscher, and Barbara Staudinger, eds. *Hofjuden und Landjuden: Jüdisches Leben in der Frühen Neuzeit.* Berlin, 2004.

Holzmüller, Johann. "Königklicher Eintritt vnd Empfang." In *Beschreibung des feierlichen Einzuges des Königs Matthias in die Stadt Wien im Jahre 1608,* Albert Camesina, 124–32. [Vienna, 1866].

Institut für Realienkunde des Mittelalters, ed. *Object Links—Dinge in Beziehung.* Formate – Forschungen zur Materiellen Kultur, vol. 1. Vienna, 2019.

Katz, Jacob. *Tradition and Crisis: Jewish Society at the End of the Middle Ages.* New York, 1993.

Keil, Martha. "Synagoge, Mikwe, Fleischbank: Die mittelalterlichen Judenviertel in Wien und Wiener Neustadt." *Österreich: Geschichte—Literatur—Geographie,* year 60, no. 3 (2016), 265–77.

Keil, Martha. "What happened to the 'New Christians'? The 'Viennese Geserah' of 1420/21 and the Forced Baptism of the Jews." In *Jews and Christians in Medieval Europe: The Historiographical Legacy of Bernhard Blumenkranz.* Religion and Law in Medieval Christian and Muslim Societies, edited by Philippe Buc, Martha Keil, and John Tolan, vol. 7, 97–114. Turnhout, 2016.

Kühtreiber, Thomas. "Die Ausgrabungen in der Alten Universität in Wien (1997–2002)." PhD diss., University of Vienna, 2006.

Kunsthalle Wien, ed. *Judenplatz Wien 1996: Wettbewerb, Mahnmal und Gedenkstätte für die jüdischen Opfer des Naziregimes in Österreich 1938–1945.* Vienna, 1996. Exhibition catalogue.

Landau Alfred, Bernhard Wachstein. *Jüdische Privatbriefe aus dem Jahre 1619.* Quellen und Forschungen zur Geschichte der Juden in Deutsch-Österreich, vol. 3. Vienna, 1911.

Lipton, Sara. *Dark Mirror: The Medieval Origins of Anti-Jewish Iconography.* New York, 2014.

Lohrmann, Klaus. *Die Wiener Juden im Mittelalter.* Geschichte der Juden in Wien, vol. 1. Berlin, 2000.

Lohrmann, Klaus. *Judenrecht und Judenpolitik im mittelalterlichen Österreich.* Handbuch zur Geschichte der Juden in Österreich, series B, vol. 1. Vienna, 1990.

Lohrmann, Klaus, ed. *1000 Jahre österreichisches Judentum.* Studia Judaica Austriaca, vol. 9. Eisenstadt, 1982.

Milchram, Gerhard, ed. *Judenplatz: Ort der Erinnerung.* Vienna, 2000.

Milchram, Gerhard, ed. *Über das Mittelalter.* Wiener Jahrbuch für jüdische Geschichte, Kultur und Museumswesen, vol. 4. Vienna, 1999/2000.

Mitchell, Paul, "Topographie und Infrastruktur des Judenviertels im spätmittelalterlichen Wien." In *Inter Judeos—Topographie und Infrastruktur jüdischer Quartiere im Mittelalter.* Erfurter Schriften zur Jüdischen Geschichte, edited by Maria Stürzebecher and Simon Paulus, vol. 5, 54–63. Erfurt, 2019.

Mitchell, Paul and Doris Schön. "Zu ebener Erde und im ersten Stock: Die Bauforschung der Stadtarchäologie Wien im Misrachi-Haus." *Perspektiven* 6/7 (2000), 61–64.

Neubauer, Adolf and Moritz Stern. *Hebräische Berichte über die Judenverfolgungen während der Kreuzzüge.* Quellen zur Geschichte der Juden in Deutschland, vol. 2. Berlin, 1892.

Nirenberg, David. *Anti-Judaism: The Western Tradition.* New York, 2013.

Pohanka, Reinhard. "Der Judenplatz nach 1421." *Perspektiven* 6/7 (2000), 37–42.

Pribram, Alfred Francis. *Urkunden und Akten zur Geschichte der Juden in Wien: Erste Abteilung, allgemeiner Teil 1526–1847 (1849).* Quellen und Forschungen zur Geschichte der Juden in Deutsch-Österreich, vol. 8. Vienna, 1918.

Rauscher, Peter, ed., assisted by Barbara Staudinger. *Austria Judaica: Quellen zur Geschichte der Juden in Niederösterreich und Wien 1496–1671.* Quelleneditionen des Instituts für Österreichische Geschichtsforschung, vol. 7. Vienna, 2011.

Sapir Abulafia, Anna. *Christian-Jewish Relations 1000–1300: Jews in the Service of Medieval Christendom.* The Medieval World. Harlow, 2011.

Scherer, Johann Egid. *Die Rechtsverhältnisse der Juden in den deutsch-österreichischen Ländern.* Beiträge zur Geschichte des Judenrechts im Mittelalter, vol. 1. Leipzig, 1901.

Schwarz, Arthur Zacharias. "Aus der Briefsammlung Sebastian Tengnagels." *Zeitschrift für hebräische Bibliographie* 20 (1917), 72–76.

Schwarz, Ignaz. *Das Wiener Ghetto, seine Häuser und seine Bewohner*. Quellen und Forschungen zur Geschichte der Juden in Deutsch-Österreich, vol. 2. Vienna, 1909.

Schön, Doris. "Von spätmittelalterlichen Mauern, renaissancezeitlichen Fenstern und barocken Fußböden: Bauforschung im Haus Wien 1, Judenplatz 8." In vol. 6 of *Fundort Wien: Berichte zur Archäologie*, 96–139. Vienna, 2003.

Shatzmiller, Joseph. *Shylock Reconsidered: Jews, Moneylending and Medieval Society*. Berkeley, 1990.

Sirat, Colette. "10 June 1386: Hannah bat Menahem Zion finished her copy of the Sefer Mitzwot Qatan." In *Bibliotheca Rosenthaliana: Treasures of Jewish Booklore—Marking the 200th Anniversary of the Birth of Leeser Rosenthal*. Edited by Adriaan K. Offenberg, Emile G. L. Schrijver, F. J. Hoogewoud, and Lies Kruijer-Poesiat, 6–7. Amsterdam, 1994.

Spitzer, Shlomo. *Bne Chet: Die österreichischen Juden im Mittelalter—Eine Sozial- und Kulturgeschichte*. Vienna, 1997.

Staub, Franz , ed. *Quellen zur Geschichte der Stadt Wien, Abt. III/I, Grundbücher der Stadt Wien, Die ältesten Kaufbücher (1368–1388)*. Vienna, 1898.

Toch, Michael. *Die Juden im mittelalterlichen Reich*. Enzyklopädie deutscher Geschichte, vol. 44. 3rd ed. Munich, 2013.

Veran, Traude. *Das steinerne Archiv: Der alte Judenfriedhof in der Rossau*. Vienna, 2002.

Wachstein, Bernhard. *Hebräische Grabsteine aus dem XIII.–XV. Jahrhundert in Wien und Umgebung* (Sitzungsberichte der Kaiserlichen Akademie der Wissenschaften 181/1). Vienna, 1916.

Wachstein, Bernhard. *Die Inschriften des alten Judenfriedhofes in Wien*, 2 vols. Quellen und Forschungen zur Geschichte der Juden in Deutsch-Österreich, vol. 4. Vienna, 1912–1917.

Wiedl, Birgit. "Laughing at the Beast—The *Judensau*: Anti-Jewish Propaganda and Humor from the Middle Ages and Early Modern Period." In *Laughter in the Middle Ages and Early Modern Times: Epistemology of a Fundamental Human Behavior, its Meaning, and Consequences*. Fundamentals of Medieval and Early Modern Culture, edited by Albrecht Classen, vol. 5, 325–64. Berlin, 2010.

Wiesenthal, Simon, ed. *Projekt: Judenplatz Wien—Zur Konstruktion von Erinnerung*. Vienna, 2000.

Zeppezauer-Wachauer, Katharina. *Kurzwîl als Entertainment: Das Mittelalterfest als popkulturelle Mittelalterrezeption—Historisch-ethnografische Betrachtungen zum Event als Spiel*. Studien zur Unterhaltungswissenschaft, vol. 6. Marburg, 2012.

List of abbreviations

BayHStA	Main Archive of the Bavarian State (Germany)
DOZA	Central Archive of the Teutonic Order
IKG	The Jewish Community of Vienna
IMAREAL	The Institute for Medieval and Early Modern Material Culture, University of Salzburg
JMW	Jewish Museum Vienna
MA 34 Wien	Municipal Department for Building and Facility Management, Vienna
MA 41 Wien	Municipal Department for Surveying and Mapping, Vienna
ÖNB	Austrian National Library
OeStA/HHStA	Austrian State Archives / Haus-, Hof- und Staatsarchiv
OeStA/FHKA	Austrian State Archives / Allgemeines Verwaltungsarchiv - Finanz- und Hofkammerarchiv
WStLA	Municipal and Provincial Archives of Vienna

Picture credits

Danielle Spera
"A contribution in the fight against forgetting"
Judenplatz: a place where past, present, and future come together

p. 6: Courtesy of 7reasons Medien GmbH

p. 9: State and University Library Hamburg, *Sidur minhag Ashkenaz ha-maaravi*, Cod. hebr. 37, fol. 27v, http://resolver.sub.uni-hamburg.de/goobi/PPN846939428, CC BY-SA 4.0

p. 10: Photo: Albert Hilscher, © ÖNB Wien: ÖGZ H 3183; Vienna City Library, Tagblattarchiv / Fotosammlung, TF 006002

p. 12: Photo: SCHNEIDER H. / APA / picturedesk.com, ID number: 19960805_PD0088

p. 13: © HGM

p. 14: Courtesy of Herbert Peter/art*uum* architecture, 2020

p. 16: Photo: Danielle Spera, 2020

p. 19: Photo: Hans Klaus Techt / APA / picturedesk.com, ID number: 20001025_PD0403

Astrid Peterle
Forward from the Present to the Past
The new permanent exhibition at Museum Judenplatz

p. 20: Skeleton of a dog, WIEN MUSEUM, inv. no. MV 21.749
Photo: Sigrid Czeika, 2005

p. 23: Key, iron, 2 × 6.5 × 12 cm
WIEN MUSEUM, inv. no. MV 25.174/335
Photo: Nafez Rerhuf, 2020

p. 25: Courtesy of Herbert Peter/art*uum* architecture, 2020

p. 27: Comb, bone, 0.4 × 5 × 11.5 cm
WIEN MUSEUM, inv. no. MV 44.752

Toy horse, ceramic, 2 × 3.5 × 5.5 cm
WIEN MUSEUM, inv. no. MV 21.206/660

Stylus, bronze, iron, 1.5 × 1.8 × 5.4 cm
WIEN MUSEUM, inv. no. MV 25.174/175

Mirror frame panels, bone, c. 0.3 × 2 × 5 cm
WIEN MUSEUM, inv. no. MV 25.176/2 und inv. no. MV 25.176/70

Photo: Nafez Rerhuf, 2020

p. 30: Courtesy of PLANET architects

p. 33: Photo: Nafez Rerhuf, 2020

Anna Lidor-Osprian
Vienna's Jewish Community in the Middle Ages

p. 34: OeStA/FHKA AHK VDA Urbare 1067B fol. 109

p. 37: © bpk | British Library Board, Add. Ms. 14762, fol. 7v

p. 38: OeStA/HHStA UR AUR 1458

p. 41: University Library Leipzig, Vollers 1102-I, fol. 131r

p. 43: © bpk | British Library Board, Add. Ms. 14762, fol. 6r

p. 45: Column fragment, lime sandstone, diameter 8 cm, height 10.5 cm
WIEN MUSEUM, inv. no. MV 25.171/67

Column base fragment, lime sandstone, 15 × 15 × 15 cm
WIEN MUSEUM, inv. no. MV 25.171/53

Photo: Nafez Rerhuf, 2020

Paul Mitchell
Judenplatz and the Former Jewish Quarter
Archaeology and building research since 1995

p. 46, 48, 51: Photos: Stadtarchäologie Wien (Vienna City Archaeology)

p. 49: Photo: Nafez Rerhuf, 2020

p. 52: (above): Photo: Nafez Rerhuf, 2020, with special thanks to Restaurant Bodega Marqués

p. 52: (below): Photo: Nafez Rerhuf, 2020, with special thanks to MA 34 Vienna

p. 54: Map: Paul Mitchell, basis: MA 41 Vienna, Stadtarchäologie Wien (Vienna City Archaeology), monument researcher: Maximilian Goriany

p. 56: Upper part of a lamp, glass, fragment 1: 4 × 2 cm, fragment 2: 2.5 × 2.5 cm
WIEN MUSEUM, inv. no. MV 25.182/321

Lower part of a lamp, glass, diameter 4 cm, length 4.5 cm
WIEN MUSEUM, inv. no. MV 25.182/63

Crocket capital, sandstone, 15 × 12 × 10 cm
WIEN MUSEUM, inv. no. MV 25.171/74

Photo: Nafez Rerhuf, 2020

p. 58–59: Photo: Nafez Rerhuf, 2020

Judenplatz 8: A Jewish House with a Varied History

p. 61: Photographer unknown, courtesy of MA 34 Vienna

p. 62: Photo: Nafez Rerhuf, 2020

p. 63: Stove tile, ceramic, 25.4 × 25.7 × 6.5 cm
WIEN MUSEUM, inv. no. MV 21750
Photo: Nafez Rerhuf, 2020

Eveline Brugger / Birgit Wiedl
Jewish-Christian Cohabitation in Medieval Vienna

p. 64: Jacob Hoefnagel (1609), bird's eye view of Vienna, in Braun/Hogenberg, *Civitates Orbis Terrarum*, vol. 6. © WIEN MUSEUM / photo: Birgit und Peter Kainz, HMW 80304

p. 66: Drinking vessel, ceramic, diameter c. 11 cm, height c. 18 cm
WIEN MUSEUM, inv. no. MV 21.206/878

Jug, ceramic, diameter 12.5 cm, height 21 cm
WIEN MUSEUM, inv. no. MV 21.206/2962

Photo: Nafez Rerhuf, 2020

p. 68: Photo: Birgit Wiedl

p. 69: Source: WStLA 3.1.1.U1.831, CC BY-NC-ND 4.0

p. 71: Die, bone, cube, side length c. 0.8 cm
WIEN MUSEUM, inv. no. MV 25.176/32

Die, bone, cube, side length c. 0.9 cm
WIEN MUSEUM, inv. no. MV 25.176/33

Dice, bone, cube, side length c. 0.7 cm
WIEN MUSEUM, inv. no. MV 25.176/42, inv. no. MV 25.176/67

Game token, bone, square, side length c. 2.8 cm
WIEN MUSEUM, inv. no. MV 25.176/13

Game token, bone, square, side length c. 2.7 cm
WIEN MUSEUM, inv. no. MV 25.176/64

Game token, bone, square, side length c. 2.3 cm
WIEN MUSEUM, inv. no. MV 25.176/69

Photo: Nafez Rerhuf, 2020

p. 72: Fish bones, WIEN MUSEUM, inv. no. MV 62.210/254/1
Photo: Nafez Rerhuf, 2020

p. 73: DOZA, inv. no. 2371

Mysterious Tokens: Coin-Like Lead Objects from the Synagogue Courtyard

p. 75: Token, lead, diameter 2.1 cm
WIEN MUSEUM, inv. no. MV 25.175/161

Token, lead, diameter 3 cm
WIEN MUSEUM, inv. no. MV 25.175/163

Token, lead, diameter 2.6 cm
WIEN MUSEUM, inv. no. MV 25.175/164

Token, lead, diameter 3.6 cm
WIEN MUSEUM, inv. no. MV 25.175/171

Token, lead, diameter 3.2 cm
WIEN MUSEUM, inv. no. MV 25.175/176

Token, lead, diameter 2.8 cm
WIEN MUSEUM, inv. no. MV 25.175/179

Token, lead, diameter 3.8 cm
WIEN MUSEUM, inv. no. MV 25.175/183

Lead seal, diameter 2.1 cm
WIEN MUSEUM, inv. no. MV 25.175/189

Photo: Nafez Rerhuf, 2020

p. 76–77: Austrian pfennig, c. 1406–1411, silver, diameter 1.6 cm
WIEN MUSEUM, inv. no. MV 25.175/139

Denar, c. 1172–1182, copper, diameter 2.2 cm
WIEN MUSEUM, inv. no. MV 25.175/165

Viennese pfennig, c. 1236–1251, silver, diameter 1.8 cm
WIEN MUSEUM, inv. no. MV 25.175/202

Viennese pfennig, c. 1236–1251, silver, diameter 1.6 cm
WIEN MUSEUM, inv. no. MV 25.175/144

Viennese pfennig (contemporary counterfeit), c. 1300–1400, bronze, diameter 1.3 cm
WIEN MUSEUM, inv. no. MV 25.175/192

Viennese pfennig, c. 1314–1330, silver, diameter 1.5 cm
WIEN MUSEUM, inv. no. MV 25.175/182

Austrian hälbling, c. 1314–1330, silver, diameter 1.1 cm
WIEN MUSEUM, inv. no. MV 25.175/181

Pfennig from Brno mint, c. 1400–1450, metal, diameter 1.4 cm
WIEN MUSEUM, inv. no. MV 25.175/184

Photo: Nafez Rerhuf, 2020

Martha Keil
Hansüß, Rifka, Joseppin: Women in the Medieval Jewish Quarter

p. 78: University and State Library Darmstadt, Cod-Or-8 Israel ben Meir, *Pesach Haggadah*, fol. 48v

p. 80: © ÖNB Wien, Cod. Hebr. 218, fol. 1r (E. 18.242-D)

p. 81: BayHStA, Reichsstadt Regensburg Urkunden 3044

p. 85: Courtesy of the City of Zurich, Office for Urban Development, Archaeology

p. 86–87: Photo: Nafez Rerhuf, 2020

Who Wrote Manuscripts in the Middle Ages? Hannah bat Menahem: an Example of a Female Scribe

p. 89: Allard Pierson, University of Amsterdam, Hs. Ros. 558, fol. 272r

Thomas Kühtreiber
May the Impure Serve to Clean

p. 90: A late medieval jug in the form of a Jew, found in Krems an der Donau
Jug (aquamanile), ceramic, 17.5 cm
museumkrems, inv. no. 1235
Photo: IMAREAL / Peter Böttcher

p. 92: University Library Graz, USB Ms 0130, fol. 30v

p. 94: Dragon aquamanile, bronze with red glass eyes, 34 × 14.5 × 38 cm
Museum für Kunst und Gewerbe Hamburg, Stiftung für die Hamburger Kunstsammlungen, inv. no. 1959.307
Photo: Karin Kiemer

p. 95: Dragon aquamanile, bronze with red glass eyes, 34 × 14.5 × 38 cm
Museum für Kunst und Gewerbe Hamburg, Stiftung für die Hamburger Kunstsammlungen, inv. no. 1959.307
Photo: Martin Luther / Dirk Fellenberg

p. 97: museumkrems, inv. no. 1235
Photo: IMAREAL / Peter Böttcher

Gravestones: Relics, Building Material, Trophies

p. 99: Gravestone of Aharon bar Baruch, Vienna 1349, 66 × 44 × 13 cm
WIEN MUSEUM, inv. no. 13680
Photo: Nafez Rerhuf, 2020

p. 100: (above): The Municipal Archive of Wiener Neustadt, Fotothek, inv. no. 24088

p. 100: (below): Photo: Bernhard Schindler, 2020

p. 101: Courtesy of Schottenstift Vienna, Library, Fragm. Hebr. 21 [Cod. 133 (Hübl 197), fol. I]

Martha Keil, Klaus Lohrmann, Simon Neuberg, Petr Elbel / Wolfram Ziegler
Q&A on the Vienna Gesera
Four perspectives on the history of the expropriation, expulsion, and murder of the Viennese Jewish community in 1420/21

p. 102: The Bodleian Library, University of Oxford, MS. Opp. 714, fol. 54v-55r

Wise Stones Falling into a Sea of Doubt
An installation about the 1420/21 Vienna Gesera by Andrew M. Mezvinsky

p. 111: Stills from *Wise Stones Falling into a Sea of Doubt*, Andrew M. Mezvinsky, 2015/2020

Nora Berend
Anti-Jewish Stereotypes from the Middle Ages until Today

p. 112: National Archives UK, inv. no. E 401/1565

p. 117: Photo: IMAREAL/Peter Böttcher

p. 118: JMW/Schlaff Collection, inv. no. 11.392

p. 121: Screenshot: APA / picturedesk.com, ID number: 20120820_PD0998

Siegrid Schmidt
From *Der kleine Ritter Trenk* to *Game of Thrones*
The Middle Ages for all age groups

p. 122: © 2015 BLUE EYES / DOR FILM

p. 125: Photo: Britta Pedersen / dpa / picturedesk.com, ID number: 20101206_PD2619

p. 126: Courtesy of Everett Collection / picturedesk.com, ID number: 20110627_PD5632

p. 127: © Everett Collection / picturedesk.com, ID number: 20140328_PD8675

p. 128: CC BY-SA 3.0 Alexander Z, Wikimedia Commons

p. 131: Photo: Liam McBurney / PA / picturedesk.com, ID number: 20190410_PD15852

Domagoj Akrap
From "Kammergut" to "Hofbefreiung"
Jews in Vienna in the early modern era

p. 132: OeStA/HHStA AUR UK. 1403V24

p. 136: OeStA/HHStA Auersperg V-B-28-13

p. 137: *Beschreibung des feierlichen Einzuges des Königs Mathias in die Stadt Wien im Jahre 1608* von Albert Camesina Ritter von San Vittore, no date, 405454-C, Table II, illustration 11 (extract), http://data.onb.ac.at/rep/10266B52 (October 30, 2020), ÖNB Wien

p. 138–39: Photo: Nafez Rerhuf, 2020

p. 141: OeStA/FHKA AHK NÖHA W 61/C/43/B fol. 424r

p. 142: Photo: Nafez Rerhuf, 2020

p. 143: OeStA/HHStA HausA Familienakten 99-49, Konv. Reichsämter und Hofämter

p. 144: © ÖNB Wien, Cod. Hebr. 30 HAN MAG, fol. 1v

A Sack Full of Letters: Insights into Everyday Jewish Life in 1619

p. 147: OeStA/HHStA Cod. Suppl. 1174, Brief Nr. 1

p. 148–49: Photo: Nafez Rerhuf, 2020

The Lessing Monument on Judenplatz: A Story from the Turbulent Twentieth Century

p. 151: Photo: Nafez Rerhuf, 2020

Astrid Peterle
Judenplatz
Biography of an urban space

p. 152: JMW / Berger Collection, inv. no. 22.111

p. 154: Photos: Nafez Rerhuf, 2020

p. 157: JMW / IKG Collection, inv. no. 4203

p. 158: JMW / JMW Collection, inv. no. 14.330/4

p. 159: Photo: Franz Hulan, source: WStLA 3.3.5.FC.7017/164, CC BY-NC-ND 4.0

p. 160: Photo: Votava / Imagno / picturedesk.com

p. 161: Photo: Ulrich Schnarr / APA Picturedesk, ID number: 19960730_PD0546

p. 162–63: Photo: Nafez Rerhuf, 2020

p. 164: JMW / JMW Collection, inv. no. 28.102

p. 165: Photo: Nafez Rerhuf, 2020

p. 166: Photo: Votava / Imagno / picturedesk.com

Authors

Domagoj Akrap has been a curator at the Jewish Museum Vienna since 2017 and also works as a librarian. He graduated from the University of Vienna in 2004 with a doctoral degree in Jewish studies and Slavonic studies and continues to work there as a lecturer at the Institute for Jewish Studies, publishing several articles on Jewish thinkers, as well as the monograph *Erich Fromm—ein jüdischer Denker* (Vienna 2011). His research focuses on Jewish cultural and intellectual history, especially Jewish mysticism and Kabbalah, Jewish thought (mainly twentieth century), Jewish book history, and Hebrew letterpress printing.

Nora Berend has been professor of European history at Cambridge University since 2018. She studied medieval history at Eötvös Loránd University (Budapest), EHESS (Paris), and Columbia University (New York). She was a research fellow at St Catharine's College Cambridge from 1996 to 1999, university lecturer at Goldsmiths College London, and then at Cambridge University. Her numerous publications include *At the Gate of Christendom: Jews, Muslims and "Pagans" in Medieval Hungary (c. 1000 – c. 1300)*. She was a visiting professor in Kyoto, Paris, and Stockholm, held a Humboldt Research Fellowship at Mannheim (2012–13), and was a fellow of the K. Hamburger Kolleg Bochum (2013–14). Awards include the Royal Historical Society's Gladstone Prize (2002), the American Association for the Study of Hungarian History's Book Prize (2003), and an honorary doctorate from the University of Stockholm (2018).

Mika Boros has been in charge of the WIEN MUSEUM coin collection since 2018. She studied archaeology and numismatics at the University of Vienna. Her special research fields include medieval and modern numismatics and the economic history of Austria.

Eveline Brugger has been a researcher at the Institute for Jewish History in Austria since 1995. She studied history and Romance studies and graduated from the Austrian Institute of Historical Research. In 2002 she wrote her doctoral thesis at the University of Vienna on the relationship between nobility and Jews in medieval Lower Austria. In 2015 she obtained her habilitation in medieval history. She has led several FWF projects and is a lecturer at the universities of Vienna, Salzburg, and Klagenfurt. Research focuses include medieval Jewish history, the economic and social history of the Middle Ages, and auxiliary sciences of history.

Petr Elbel has been head of the Department of Auxiliary Historical Sciences and Archive Studies at the University of Brno since 2014. He studied history and the auxiliary sciences of history at the University of Brno. From 2004 to 2014 he worked at the Austrian Academy of Sciences Institute for Medieval Research, where he was involved in revising the collection of official documents of Emperor Sigismund and King Albert II. His research focuses are document research, late medieval history, and church history.

Alexandra Hylla has been curator of the coin and medal collection at the Salzburg Museum since 2018 and, as of 2020, editor of the magazine *Barockberichte*. She studied cultural sciences and art history at FernUniversität Hagen and LMU Munich from 2009 to 2016. In 2011 she became a research assistant for coin finds and hoards at the Bavarian State Coin Collection Munich (SMM), and from 2014 to 2017 was involved in the research and exhibition project *Geprägte Bilderwelten der Romanik* with Stiftung Bozner Schlösser, the KHM Vienna, and the SMM.

Martha Keil has been working as a researcher at the Institute for the Jewish History of Austria since 1988 and became its director in 2004. She studied history and Jewish studies in Vienna and Berlin. Since 2007 she has been a lecturer in Austrian history at the University of Vienna and in 2016 became Senior Scientist at the university's Institute of Austrian Historical Research. She has been involved in numerous research projects, publications, and exhibitions on everyday Jewish life and culture, relations with Christian society, and the history of women and gender studies in the pre-modern era, as well as the Jewish history of Austria and the culture of remembrance.

Thomas Kühtreiber is an archaeologist and cultural scientist with a focus on the Middle Ages and the modern era. He studied prehistoric and early history, ethnology, history, and earth sciences at the University of Vienna and since 1997 has been a staff member at the Institute for Medieval and Early Modern Material Culture (until 2012 Austrian Academy of Sciences, since then University of Salzburg) in Krems.

Anna Lidor-Osprian has been a research assistant for the chair of late medieval history at the Department of History of the University of Heidelberg since 2020. She was a university assistant in medieval history and a doctoral candidate at the University of Graz from 2017 until 2020. Between 2018 and 2021, she carried out research for the new permenant exhibition at Museum Judenplatz. Between 2013 and 2017 she lived and worked in Israel, where she was a teacher of German in the Austrian Academic Exchange Program (OeAD) at Ben-Gurion University in Beersheba. Focusing primarily on medieval Jewish history and culture, she is currently writing a dissertation on the cultural significance of death and the dead body in the Jewish communities of medieval Europe.

Klaus Lohrmann was associate professor of medieval history as well as founder and long-standing director of the Institute for Jewish History in Austria. For many years he was a leading member of the campaign group "Aktion gegen den Antisemitismus," serving as managing vice-president together with Wolfgang Neugebauer.

Paul Mitchell is an archaeologist and building researcher. Since 2000 he has been an independent archaeologist specializing in historical archaeology and the archaeology of buildings (working on projects such as the Hofburg Vienna, Gozzoburg Krems, Mauthausen Memorial). He has conducted archaeological digs, been involved in exhibitions, worked as a specialist translator, and written and co-authored numerous academic papers, articles, and expert studies. He studied history at the University of Manchester and worked as an archaeologist at the Museum of London (1987–1990) and the Landesdenkmalamt Baden-Württemberg (until 1995). He was a city archaeologist in Vienna (until 1999) and an employee of the Verein AS-Archäologie Service (until 2009).

Simon Neuberg has been professor of Yiddish studies at the University of Trier since 2002. After studying languages, he trained as a conference interpreter at the University of Paris III (Sorbonne Nouvelle) and graduated in 1986 from the

École supérieure d'interprètes et de traducteurs (ESIT). Since starting his formal Yiddish studies in Trier (1995 doctorate, 1999 habilitation), he has published articles (above all in German and Yiddish) on the history of Yiddish language and literature and on modern Yiddish. With Marion Aptroot (professor of Yiddish studies in Düsseldorf) he organizes the annual Symposium for Yiddish Studies in Germany.

Astrid Peterle has been curator and executive personal assistant to the CEO at the Jewish Museum Vienna since 2010 and became head curator in May 2018. She studied history and art history in Vienna, Berlin, and New York, obtaining her doctorate in 2009. She has worked as a visiting lecturer at the universities of Vienna, Graz, and Salzburg, and is curator for performance at the donaufestival. She has written numerous articles on Viennese Jewish history, cultural history, and contemporary art, in particular performance art, photography, and feminist art. Her exhibitions for the Jewish Museum Vienna include *Buy from Jews! Story of a Viennese Store Culture*, *VALIE EXPORT Intervenes*, and *Tales of 2 Cities*.

Siegrid Schmidt is an academic assistant at the Department of German Studies (Medieval Language and Literature) at the University of Salzburg. She studied German studies, music, and political science, receiving her doctorate in 1988 in attitudes to the Middle Ages in German literature after 1945. She initially obtained a research stipend at the Max Reinhardt Research and Memorial Center in Salzburg, and pursued postgraduate training in museum education, with practical experience in several museums. In 1995 she became a research assistant at the University of Salzburg. Her research interests are the *Nibelungenlied*, Middle High German and New High German fool's literature, late medieval lyricism, attitudes to the Middle Ages in literature, (music) theater in connection with the Salzburg Easter and summer festivals, literature didactics, and museology. She has edited and co-edited volumes on medieval cultural heritage, theater, and music theater.

Adina Seeger is a historian and curator; from 2015 to 2019 assistant curator, and since 2019 curator at the Jewish Museum Vienna. From 2018 to 2021 she was project coordinator and co-curator of the new permanent exhibition at Museum Judenplatz. Previously, she collaborated in historical exhibition and research projects, including the Buchenwald Memorial. Publications include articles on Nazi perpetrators and the history of the Bauhaus. Since 2016 she has been a member of the editorial board of the magazine *zeitgeschichte*. In 2018 she won the City of Vienna Prize for Public Education with Philipp Rohrbach for the Austrian Heritage Archive project.

Danielle Spera has been director of the Jewish Museum Vienna since 2010, where she has been involved in numerous cultural exhibitions and publications, including *Arik Brauer: All of my Arts*, *Andy Warhol's Jewish Geniuses*, and *Lessing presents Lessing*. She studied journalism and political science at the University of Vienna. From 1978 to 2010 she was journalist, reporter, presenter, and editorial advisor at ORF, and in 1987/88 ORF correspondent in Washington, DC. She was president of ICOM Austria from 2013 to 2019, since 2020 vice-president; from 2013 to 2018 she was a member of the University Council of the Medical University of Innsbruck. A Romy Prize winner in 1991 and 2007, she lectured at the University of Vienna Department of Communications from 1990 to 2002 and has written and published numerous books and articles on contemporary art, Jewish subjects, and for the magazine *NU*.

Birgit Wiedl has been at the Institute for Jewish History in Austria since 2000, working on a project examining historical documents on the history of the Jews in medieval Austria. She obtained her doctorate in medieval history at the University of Salzburg and an MAS in historical research and archival science from the University of Vienna. She has also headed various FWF projects. She is a lecturer at the universities of Salzburg (since 2009) and Klagenfurt (since 2017), and in 2016 obtained her habilitation in medieval history from the University of Graz. Other research focuses include economic and social history, history of anti-Judaism, and urban history.

Wolfram Ziegler has been a staff member of the parliamentary adminstration in Vienna since 2018. He studied history and auxiliary sciences of history at the University of Vienna. He worked at the WIEN MUSEUM and the Institute for Medieval Research at the Austrian Academy of Sciences and from 2012 in the parliament archive, the University of Brno, the Upper Austrian Provincial Archive, and the University of Luxembourg. His research focuses include high and late medieval history, and twentieth-century history of science and culture.

Acknowledgments

Gerhard Abel, PLANET architects
Michael Alram, Austrian Academy of Sciences/Kunsthistorisches Museum Vienna
Anna Artaker
Mika Boros, WIEN MUSEUM
Michael Brenner, LMU Munich
Matti Bunzl, WIEN MUSEUM
Yvonne Burger, Mauthausen Memorial
Sigrid Czeika, Vienna City Archaeology Department
Ilse Danziger, Jewish Community Regensburg
Berthold Ecker, WIEN MUSEUM
Karin Fischer Ausserer and the entire team from the Vienna City Archaeology Department
Matthias Freitag, Culture Department/City of Regensburg
Rahel Fronda, The Bodleian Libraries
Aleksandra und Stefan Fuhrer, Fuhrer, Vienna
Alfred Galik, Austrian Academy of Sciences
Christian Ganzer, ZOOM Kindermuseum
Karina Grömer, Natural History Museum Vienna
Dominikus Guggenberger
Saskia Haag
Claudia Haas
Michael Häupl
Heidrun Helgert, Vienna City Archaeology Department
Hilfsgemeinschaft der Blinden und Sehschwachen Österreichs (Andrea Hutter, Daniele Marano, Christian Vogelauer)
Sabine Hödl, Institute for Jewish History in Austria
Alexandra Hylla, Salzburg Museum
Maria Grundner, Mobilitätsagentur Wien
Rifka Junger
Thomas Just, Austrian State Archives/Haus-, Hof- und Staatsarchiv
Dawit Kassaw, PLANET architects
Martha Keil, Institute for Jewish History in Austria
Hannes Köcher, cat-x exhibitions
Harald Krejci, Belvedere Vienna
Michaela Kronberger, WIEN MUSEUM
Thomas Kühtreiber, Institute for Medieval and Early Modern Material Culture, University of Salzburg
Daniela Laudehr, Culture Department/City of Regensburg
Sylvie Liska
Klaus Lohrmann, University of Vienna
Christina Lutter, University of Vienna
Peter Marboe
Andrew M. Mezvinsky
Gerhard Milchram, WIEN MUSEUM
Betti Moser
Martin Mosser, Vienna City Archaeology Department
Raw Pardess, Mizrachi Austria
Ursula Pasterk
Verena Pawlowsky
Herbert Peter, art*uum* architecture

Roland Plachy
Reinhard Pohanka
Florian Prix, cat-x exhibitions
Christian Rapp, Haus der Geschichte – Museum Niederösterreich
Nafez Rerhuf
Vera Ribarich
Astrid Riedler-Pohlers
Markus Roboch, Natural History Museum Vienna
Andreas Rohatsch, TU Vienna
Katja Schmitz von Ledebur, Kunsthistorisches Museum Vienna
Doris Schön
Archbishop Cardinal Christoph Schönborn
Horst Seiwerth
Nick Somers
Maria Stürzebecher, Old Synagogue/City of Erfurt
Kinga Tarcsay, Vienna City Archaeology Department
Robert Tauber, Austrian Broadcasting Corporation (ORF)
Patrick Topitschnig
Christiane Twiehaus, MiQua Cologne
Alexandra Verdeil, Tactile Studio
Viktoria Wagesreiter, WIEN MUSEUM
Karlheinz Wagner
Guenther Weinlinger, 7reasons Medien GmbH, Vienna
Rachel Whiteread
Wolfram Ziegler, Austrian Academy of Sciences

For their generous support, we would like to thank:

Chamber for Workers and Employees Vienna
feratel media technologies AG
Friends of the Jewish Museum Vienna
Hausservice Objektbewirtschaftungs GmbH
Münze Österreich AG (Austrian Mint)
National Fund of the Republic of Austria for Victims of National Socialism
NITSCH FOUNDATION
Ottakringer Getränke AG
pancivis stiftung
Rothschild Foundation Hanadiv Europe
Mark and Melissa Simon in memory of their great-grandfather Osias "Oskar" Steinfeld
Prof. Stefan Stolitzka
US Friends of the Jewish Museum Vienna
Zumtobel Group

making
vienna
worth
living.
Your life is our passion.
Culture, real estate, logistics and media:
Wien Holding brings our city to life.
Wherever and whenever you want.
365 days a year. For everyone in Vienna.
www.wienholding.at
making vienna worth living.
wienholding
The company of the City of Vienna
GGK MULLENLOWE

Raiffeisen Wien
Meine Stadtbank
NUR WER ZUHÖRT,
KANN ECHT HELFEN.
WIR MACHEN DEN UNTERSCHIED.
Impressum: Medieninhaber: Raiffeisenlandesbank Niederösterreich-Wien AG, F.-W.-Raiffeisen-Platz 1, 1020 Wien.

AK KUNSTPROJEKTE

Foto © Hertha Hurnaus

kultur.arbeiterkammer.at

AK WIEN

Sotheby's EST. 1744
Know Your Worth.
Sotheby's Valuations Services provide bespoke valuations across all collecting categories that are recognised around the world by financial institutions, insurance brokers and government agencies.
34–35 NEW BOND STREET, LONDON W1A 2AA
ENQUIRIES +44 (0)20 7293 6422 VALUATIONS@SOTHEBYS.COM
SOTHEBYS.COM/VALUATIONS #SOTHEBYSVALUATIONS
© DOUGLAS MACKIE © SIMON UPTON © THE ESTATE OF ADRIAN HEATH
DOWNLOAD SOTHEBY'S APP
FOLLOW US @SOTHEBYS

Mit Sicherheit
in besten Händen.
Fullservice für Ihren Kulturbetrieb
Aufsichtsdienste & Objektschutz
Kassen- & Shopdienste
Garderobenservice
Kuvertierung
Eventbetreuung
MUS
ORG
Sicherheitsdienstleistungen und
Museumsorganisation
www.musorg.at

REIN INS
MITTELALTER.
Das Team von da-ka reinigt Tag für Tag nicht
nur das neue Wien, sondern auch das alte.
da-ka
Hausbetreuung - Gebäudereinigung
www.da-ka.at

Raiffeisen
Meine Bank
INVESTING
FOR GOOD.
Socially responsible investment means investing in companies that apply environmentally friendly business practices, offer fair working conditions, and provide transparent information about how and where your capital is invested. Because it does make a difference where you choose to invest your money – and you can do good things with the SRI funds at your Raiffeisen bank. For more information, visit blog.raiffeisenfonds.at
Investments in funds are subject to the risk of price fluctuations and capital losses.
Produced by: Raiffeisen Kapitalanlage-Gesellschaft m.b.H., Mooslackengasse 12, 1190 Vienna, Austria, as of September 2020

WEISEN HEIMER LEGAL
WEISENHEIMER LEGAL
[ˈwī-zən-ˌhī-mər]
WIR BEI WEISENHEIMER LEGAL SIND GERNE SCHLAUBERGER. WIR FINDEN, DASS SIE DIE BESTE BERATUNG VERDIENEN. JEMAND, DER SICH MIT SEINEM GESAMTEN KNOW-HOW IN IHR UNTERNEHMEN EINBRINGT UND DIE FÜR IHRE SITUATION SCHLAUESTE UND BESTE LÖSUNG FINDET. JEMAND, DER UNTERNEHMERISCH DENKT UND DIE JURISTISCHE LÖSUNG STETS AN DER WIRTSCHAFTLICHEN ZIELSETZUNG ORIENTIERT. JEMAND, DER SIE UND IHR UNTERNEHMEN KENNT UND VERSTEHT. IHR PERSÖNLICHER WEISENHEIMER.
AVIATION AND TRANSPORTATION
LEGAL PROJECT MANAGEMENT
FOUNDERS AND START UPS
CORPORATE (AND SME) FINANCING
RESTRUCTURING AND BUSINESS SUCCESSION
WWW.WEISENHEIMER.LAW
WALFISCHGASSE 8/TOP 34
1010 WIEN

Imprint

Our Medieval City! The First Jewish Community in Vienna

Published by Astrid Peterle, Adina Seeger, Domagoj Akrap, and Danielle Spera

Catalogue editors: Caitlin Gura-Redl, Agnes Meisinger

This publication appears in conjunction with the new permanent exhibition at Museum Judenplatz.

Jewish Museum Vienna
Museum Judenplatz
Judenplatz 8
1010 Vienna

www.jmw.at

Director: Danielle Spera
Project management: Astrid Peterle (head curator), Adina Seeger (project coordinator)
Curators: Astrid Peterle, Adina Seeger, Domagoj Akrap, Janine Zettl
Exhibition production: Caitlin Gura-Redl
Research assistant: Anna Lidor-Osprian
Consultant (archaeology and building research): Paul Mitchell
AR/VR installation, concept and realization: Herbert Peter/ art*uum* architecture
City model: 7reasons Medien GmbH, Vienna (Michael Klein, Alexander Kostreba, Erwin Polasek, Christian Sovis, Günther Weinlinger)
Artistic contributions: Anna Artaker, Andrew M. Mezvinsky
Illustrations: Roland Plachy
Tactile stations: Tactile Studio (Lena Becker, Alexandra Verdeil, Maxime Kosnansky, Eric Lemaresquier, Workshop WAM)
Design of educational objects: Dominikus Guggenberger
Topography of the Jewish quarter, plan and texts: Paul Mitchell
App texts on particular aspects of the excavation: Paul Mitchell, Kinga Tarcsay (no. 4), Martin Mosser (no. 15)
Tactile synagogue model: Herbert Peter/artuum architecture
Audio commentaries: Mika Boros, Sigrid Czeika, Karin Fischer Ausserer, Alfred Galik, Alexandra Hylla, Andreas Rohatsch
Educational programming: Hannah Landsmann, Julia Windegger
Conservation management: Bettina Dräxler
Cleaning and stabilization of the archaeological remains: Beate Sipek
Restoration of the floor around the excavations: mindquarters
Archive management: Christa Prokisch, Katharina Lischka
Literature research: Sabine Frank-Moser

Exhibition design: PLANET architects (Gerhard Abel, Dawit Kassaw, Fit Phuong, Manuela Patka) and Fuhrer, Vienna
Graphic design and orientation system: Fuhrer, Vienna
Translations German to English: Nick Somers
Translations English to German: Vera Ribarich
Copy-editing and proofreading German: Vera Ribarich, Verena Pawlowsky (exhibition texts), Saskia Haag (foreword, picture captions, focus texts)
Copy-editing and proofreading English: Betti Moser
Transcriptions: Elisa Heinrich
Object photography: Nafez Rerhuf

Technical management: Severin Mahrer
AR/VR installation, technical concept and realization: cat-x exhibitions (programming: Hannes Köcher; project management: Florian Doppel-Prix; team: Andreas Platzer, Claudio della Schiava)
Media: cat-x exhibitions (programming: Hannes Köcher; project management: Florian Doppel-Prix; team: Andreas Platzer, Claudio della Schiava)
AR/VR installation, engineering: der ProtoTyp (Bernhard Ranner)
Construction of the tactile synagogue model: Modellart (Michael Eisenkölbl)
Construction of the model of the Jewish quarter at Unterer Werd: Martina Berger
Animation and technical implementation of the art installation by Anna Artaker: Stefan Kainbacher (BPNXT / Vienna)
Video interviews, film editing and production (Palais Eskeles): Patrick Topitschnig
Audio commentary editing: Tom Juncker
Exhibition construction: Tischlerei Kirchberger; Martina Berger; Aumayer GmbH
Art handling: hs art service austria GmbH

Commercial management: Josef Gaschnitz, Markus Roboch (until May 2020)
Accounting: Claudia Lauppert
Registrar's office: Cornelia Regehr
Legal: Birgit Antes (until November 2020)
Building management: Behzad Haghirian, Drago Kecman, Ivica Pavljašević
PR and social media: Petra Fuchs
Sponsoring and marketing: Ida Salamon
Event management: Verena Schrom, Ida Salamon